MEMORY SEARCH
BY A MEMORIST

MEMORY SEARCH
BY A MEMORIST

Charles P. Thompson
Thaddeus M. Cowan
Jerome Frieman
Kansas State University

LEA LAWRENCE ERLBAUM ASSOCIATES, PUBLISHERS
1993   Hillsdale, New Jersey   Hove and London

Lawrence Erlbaum Associates, Inc., Publishers
365 Broadway
Hillsdale, New Jersey 07642

Library of Congress Cataloging-in-Publication Data

Thompson, Charles P.
    Memory search by a memorist / Charles P. Thompson, Thaddeus M.
Cowan, Jerome Frieman.
        p.   cm.
    Includes bibliographical references and index.
    ISBN 0-8058-1236-9
    1. Memory.   2. Memory–Case studies.   3. Mnemonics.   4. Mahadevan,
Rajan.   I. Cowan, Thaddeus M.   II. Frieman, Jerome.   III. Title.
BF371.T48   1993
153.1'2 – dc20   93-2417
                                                                              CIP

Books published by Lawrence Erlbaum Associates are printed on acid-free
paper, and their bindings are chosen for strength and durability.

Printed in the United States of America
10 9 8 7 6 5 4 3 2 1

In memory of Dorothy Thompson
Wife
And friend

Top row, left to right: Jerome Frieman, Charles P. Thompson, and Thaddeus M. Cowan. Bottom row, left to right: Rajan Srinivasan Mahadevan, Rodney Vogl.

Contents

Preface

In this brief volume, we share with you the results of our research project on Rajan Mahadevan, a man with an extraordinary skill for memorizing and recalling digits. Our goal was to understand that skill. However, Rajan was more than a research subject; we worked closely with him for 3 years and came to know him as a colleague and a friend. In our opening chapter, we attempt to describe who Rajan is and how we came to work with him.

When we first met Rajan, we did not know of his fame. It is accurate to say that he chose this project for us rather than we chose this project for him. Rajan's choices were interesting: two cognitive psychologists and a behaviorist. Charles Thompson was the obvious person to lead our research project, given that he has spent all of his professional career studying memory. On the other hand, Thaddeus Cowan's background is in perception, and his creative mind spawned a number of clever experiments reported here. Jerome Frieman's training is in operant conditioning; he brought experience with single-subject research to this project. Together we pooled our various talents and diverse knowledge to carry this project to its successful conclusion.

Usually the results of projects of this sort trickle out in the form of separate reports in learned journals, but we felt that a full account of all our studies under one cover would best embrace the intricacies of Rajan's remarkable memory. The title, descriptive as it is, perhaps was not the best put forth, however. Chuck Thompson proposed *A Slice of Rajan's pi*, but cooler heads prevailed.

Most of the book chronicles our studies of Rajan and four control subjects. Over the course of 3 years we subjected these five people to a variety of procedures. The arrangement of these chapters does not reflect the chronological order of events; instead, we attempt to organize our presentation into major themes. We believe this will make it easier for you to keep track of our findings.

We close with a brief comparison of Rajan with other memorists and a summary of what Rajan taught us. Our descriptions of these other memorists are not intended to be in depth. We refer you to the excellent chapter by Brown and Deffenbacker (1988) in L. K. Obler and D. Fein (Eds.), *The Exceptional Brain* (pp. 191–211) for more details on the lives and skills of these other memorists.

ACKNOWLEDGMENTS

This project could not have been completed without the assistance of a number of people. Our special thanks goes to Rodney Vogl, who oversaw much of the day-to-day operations of this project. Without Rod, subjects and testers might not have crossed paths, and we might not have retrieved some of the data we collected when the time came to write this volume. Rod also helped catch a number of errors in the early drafts of our manuscript.

We also received assistance from a number of other people over the course of this project. We want to acknowledge the work of Will Eckels, Cosima Hadidi, Jana Ortiz, and David Welsh, who served as testers for our subjects. Swastika Nastoff and Jeff Gibbons also helped us research some of the background information, and they reviewed drafts of this book.

John Gardner came to Manhattan for a short visit, never dreaming that he would spend much of his time reading a draft of this book. We owe John a great debt for his willingness to review our manuscript and for his insightful comments and suggestions. Likewise, our colleague Stephen Kiefer graciously reviewed portions of our manuscript and provided us with helpful comments.

Dan Aeschliman, Minida Dowdy, Tricia Hoard, and Grant Nurnberg served as our control subjects. Their task was not an easy one. We subjected them to hours of repetitive testing on some very difficult tasks. To their credit, they kept their part of the bargain and stayed with the project for as long as personal circumstances permitted. For three of them (Dan, Tricia, and Grant) this spanned the entire 3 years of the project.

Throughout this project, from its initial conception to its successful completion, we received encouragement and support from our good friend and colleague Henry L. "Roddy" Roediger III. On numerous occasions, Roddy provided us with counsel and advice.

We wish to thank Academic Press for granting us their permission to reproduce materials from our paper "Rajan: A Study of a Memorist" which appeared in the *Journal of Memory and Language*, Volume 30, No. 6, in December of 1991. We also wish to thank the American Mathematical Society for their permission to reprint the first page of the materials Rajan used to study the decimal digits of pi. These appeared in "Computation of pi to 100,000 Decimals," by Daniel Shanks and John W. Wrench, Jr., *Mathematics of Computation*, Volume 16.

The research reported here was supported by National Institute of Mental Health Grant MH44090. The reviewers of our grant proposal recognized that we not only had a unique opportunity to systematically study a unique person over an extended period of time but also that this could further our understanding of the workings of human memory. We thank them and the officials at NIMH for their support and encouragement.

— Charles P. Thompson
— Thaddeus M. Cowan
— Jerome Frieman

Rajan the Person

Rajan Srinivasan Mahadevan developed an extraordinary skill at learning and reciting long strings of digits. On July 5, 1981, he demonstrated this skill by reciting the first 31,811 digits of pi to earn a place in the *Guinness Book of World Records*. That record stood until March 9, 1987 when another memorist (Hideaki Tomoyori) recited 40,000 digits of pi.

In addition to his memory skills, Rajan is an interesting and rather eccentric fellow. We had the opportunity to interact with Rajan virtually every day for 4 years. He is absolutely delightful in many ways and somewhat exasperating in others.

In this book, our main purpose is to document his exceptional performance in the laboratory with data we collected over a 3-year period. We think the reader will agree that his laboratory performance is much more impressive than his recitation of pi.

Before we begin that task, we describe Rajan the person. This first chapter portrays many of the characteristics that define his rich and unique personality. We begin with a brief autobiography provided by Rajan.

FAMILY AND EARLY LIFE

Rajan's Autobiography

I was born in Madras, India, in 1957. Two years later, my family moved to Mangalore as a consequence of my father securing a professorship at the medical school there.

The earliest evidence of my unusual memory was furnished at age 5 when my parents hosted a party for about 50 guests. Being somewhat restless by nature, I embarked on a small tour of the nearest parking lot and submitted the license plate of every guest to close scrutiny. Several minutes later, I returned to my living room and reproduced the license plate number of every guest in the order the vehicles were parked.

Although our guests were impressed with my license plate number mastery, my memory skills never merited any serious consideration from my teachers or my colleagues throughout my early schooling. Their indifference could be attributed at least partially to the fact that I hailed from a predominantly academic family, with many members earning a reputation for strong memory skills.

Throughout my schooling, I used to entertain people by reproducing railway timetables and cricket scores. I recall a particular incident that occurred when I was in Grade 4. Our instructor cited several reasons to demonstrate the safety of railroad travel in India. Somewhat piqued, I got up and gave the class several details of railroad accidents in India over the previous decade (I was able to relive that experience when I watched the movie, *Rain Man*, in which Dustin Hoffman reproduced, from memory, the data on airplane accidents to Tom Cruise).

In the fall of 1975, I enrolled at the engineering school at Manipal. It was there that people showed considerable curiosity at my numerical memory. Several people urged me to set a world record for memorizing numbers. I wrote to the editors of the *Guinness Book of World Records* and they advised me to focus on pi. Pi is a well-known mathematical constant and was chosen as the yardstick to measure numerical memory.

I discontinued my engineering education in 1977 (primarily due to a waning of my interest in the field), after which I procured a computer listing of the digits of pi. I had memorized the first 10,000 digits by the time I was invited to demonstrate my memory skills at an international conference on yoga and meditation held in Chicago in 1980.

At the conclusion of the conference, I visited friends at Minnesota. They suggested that a psychologist test my memory, and they contacted a cognitive psychologist, Bill Fox, at the University of Minnesota. Fox put me through an extensive series of tests over a 3-month period. Those tests revealed quite clearly that my memory was predominantly numerical with a vast variation in performance depending on the type of material and the task demands.

On my return to India in early 1981, I enrolled as a psychology major at the School of Social Work in Mangalore. Later that year, I memorized an additional 25,000 digits of pi. On July 5th, 1981, I reproduced 31,811 digits of pi flawlessly and entered the *Guinness Book of World Records*.

I completed my Bachelor's degree in psychology in 1984 and received my Master's degree in clinical psychology from the University of Mysore in 1986. My memory was tested periodically by my instructors during the 5-year period from 1981–1986. The results were generally consistent with Fox's findings in 1980.

Although my skill is predominantly with numbers, I consider myself as having a good memory for verbal material as well. I can attest to this fact by demonstrating fluency and reasonable accuracy in a dozen languages.

I enrolled as a graduate student in physiological psychology at Kansas State University in the fall of 1987. At Kansas State, a research project was funded in early 1989 to probe the characteristics of my memory. The results of that research constitute the major part of this book.

Rajan and Ramanujan

An interesting addition to Rajan's autobiography is the origin of his given name, Srinivasan. He is named after a distant cousin who perhaps was India's most famous mathematician, Srinivasa Ramanujan. Ramanujan was a man for whom it was claimed that every number was a personal friend. A widely circulated story (Newman, 1956) tells how Ramanujan's mentor, G. H. Hardy, remarked in passing that the license number of a certain taxi, 1729, was a particularly dull number. Ramanujan quickly pointed out that it was an interesting number because it was the smallest number expressible as a sum of two cubes in two different ways. In a poem about Ramanujan, Holden (1985) stated that:

This modest, mousy little boy from India
could reel off pi's digits to any
decimal place his classmates dared him to.
No mean feat. But for Ramanujan it
was a breeze. Pi was merely one of his
first cousins, in fact a favorite.
And his cousins were innumerable.

It is doubtful that Ramanujan's playmates ever challenged him with decimal places as remote as those held by one of his mortal cousins, Rajan.

ORIGIN OF THIS PROJECT

Entering Kansas State University

Our part of the story begins in late August of 1987 when Rajan introduced himself to each of us. He was then 30 years old and had just begun graduate work in our department. Rajan's initial meeting with Charles Thompson demonstrated a central theme in his personality and also led directly to our research project:

Rajan walked into my office, introduced himself, and said that he was a new graduate student in psychology. I welcomed him to the department and said that I hoped he would have an enjoyable and profitable stay with us. I then asked him what areas of psychology interested him. He replied that he was interested in memory. I said something like, "That's great! My specialty is memory. Is there any particular topic in memory that interests you?" "Yes," he replied, "my memory." My thoughts upon hearing that reply were not completely charitable. Nonetheless, I asked what there was about his memory that made it of particular interest to him. Rajan went on to describe some of his memory feats with particular focus on his recitation of almost 32,000 digits of pi. The performance he described was very impressive. Rajan mentioned he had chatted with two of my colleagues (Thad Cowan and Jerry Frieman) and they were both intrigued with his memory skills.

It seemed clear to me that it was worth investing a bit of time to establish whether he had the skills he described. Shortly after my meeting with Rajan, Thad Cowan, Jerry and Jeanne Frieman, and I discussed Rajan at Max Miller's traditional pre-Labor Day party at beautiful Lake Wabaunsee. I asked whether they would be interested in evaluating Rajan's skilled performance. This book testifies to their response.

Rajan's meeting with Thompson was typical of other initial meetings that we observed or had described to us. In virtually every case, Rajan made the description or demonstration of his memory skill the central feature of the conversation. That characterization seems unkind until one considers all the people one knows who are adept at turning almost all conversations to topics in which they are interested and have expertise. The defining differences between those people and Rajan are that their topics do not usually depend on their personal performance, and their expertise is not quite so startling.

More importantly, it appeared to us that Rajan found focusing the conversation on his memory skill an easy way to get through an introduction with grace and charm. Once he mentions his expertise to someone who does not know him, the questions tumble out like oranges from an upset basket. Because the questions are all fairly predictable, Rajan can answer them with the fluency and skill of a great story teller.

As we observed Rajan's interactions with others, it became clear to us that his memory skill was the central defining feature of his view of himself. At first, that perspective seemed somewhat eccentric to us; however, his behavior became very understandable when we were made aware of the immense amount of attention that Rajan has received as a direct result of his memory performances.

Initial Tests

Our individual meetings with Rajan convinced us that it was worth the effort to determine what his performance looked like under controlled laboratory conditions. We chose memory span and recitation of the decimal digits of pi as our initial tests.

Memory span is a simple test in which a string of digits is presented at a rate of one digit per second. At the end of the presentation, the subject is asked to recite the string in the order presented. The length of the string is increased by one if the recitation is correct and is decreased by one if the subject makes an error. After 10 or 20 trials, performance stabilizes, with subjects usually able to recite strings of a given length but failing when the strings are one digit longer. The memory span for adults is remarkably stable with a typical span of seven. Deviations of more than two digits from that level are extremely rare. We quickly were able to establish that Rajan's digit span was about 40 digits. We obviously were dealing with an individual who was extremely skilled at recalling digit strings.

Rajan's performance in reciting pi was equally impressive. We made a videotape of him reciting the first 8,000 digits of pi. Both his accuracy and his speed were impressive: He made no errors while reciting the digits at a rate slightly greater than five digits per second. His recitation rate was so rapid that it took some practice to follow the tape in order to verify the accuracy of his performance.

Rajan's performance convinced us that we should study his memory. We needed financial support to do the extensive studies that would be necessary. Thus, we quickly submitted a grant proposal to the National Institutes of Mental Health to meet an October 1 deadline. (As one of its many functions, NIMH sponsors basic research in memory.) We paid for our haste, however, as the reviewing committee wisely asked for additional information demonstrating his expertise prior to funding our grant.

As part of our response, we submitted our videotape of Rajan reciting the first 8,000 digits of pi. We heard, both directly and indirectly, that the committee (and others) enjoyed viewing that tape. It was difficult not to be interested in his performance. For example, the program officer in charge of processing our grant application called one day – allegedly to get some piece of information. It soon became clear, however, that she had called to chat about "that interesting young man on whom you propose to do some research."

Ethical Problems and Solutions

Our decision to use Rajan as a research subject posed several ethical problems. Most importantly, we thought that it would be inappropriate for us to interfere in any way with Rajan's progress as a graduate student. We solved that problem in two ways: First, we undertook no additional research with Rajan until the grant was funded. Second, we specified in the grant that Rajan would be funded as a graduate research assistant on the project under rather special conditions. Typically, graduate research assistants can use some of their work on the sponsored research (which pays their assistantship) to fulfill the research requirements for their degree. However, that strategy would not work for Rajan because work on oneself is wholly inappropriate for a research degree. To provide Rajan the same opportunity for research relevant to his degree as other research assistants, we specified in our grant proposal that, of the 20 hours per week normally expected of a graduate research assistant, Rajan would spend 10 hours as a subject and would be free to spend the other 10 hours on his own research.

In all other respects, Rajan benefitted from the project in the same way as any other graduate research assistant. He was coauthor on a major paper resulting from the research (Thompson, Cowan, Frieman, Mahadevan, Vogl, & Frieman, 1991) and coauthor on five paper or poster presentations.

The second problem was that Rajan had not decided whether he would pursue research in memory or in physiological psychology. If he chose memory, Charles Thompson was an obvious candidate to either serve on, or head, his committee. However, we viewed that as an unacceptable conflict of interest because Thompson had also taken the principal investigator role in the grant proposal. Therefore, we agreed that he would play no role in the research Rajan conducted for his degree.

The third problem that concerned us was the possibility that Rajan would be besieged with requests to perform in classes and elsewhere. We resolved to shield Rajan from those requests as much as possible. We soon found that our concern was misplaced. Rajan loved to perform and sought out opportunities to do so. Thus, most of our large introductory courses and most of our cognitive psychology courses had the opportunity to see Rajan perform during the period he was a graduate student at Kansas State University. Rajan also spent many hours at the Espresso Royale Caffe (a local coffee shop) giving performances to individual patrons.

INTERVIEWS

Grant Leads to Interviews

Although we were able to begin our research early in 1989, the official starting date of the grant was May 1, 1989. Shortly before that date, the publicity office at Kansas State University put out a routine bulletin describing the grant and its purpose. To our surprise, the Associated Press sent the bulletin on its wire service, and stories of the grant began to appear around the country. Those stories, in turn, led to requests for personal interviews with Rajan.

One of the earliest requests was from T. R. Reid of the *Washington Post*. He came to Kansas, interviewed Rajan, and published an entertaining story on Rajan in the *Washington Post* (Sunday, June 18, 1989). His was a very informative and influential story, which led to dozens of interviews. The *Washington Post* story was reprinted in a large number of newspapers. In January 1990, it appeared in the *Reader's Digest* and later in the Spanish language version of that magazine. The *Washington Post* story apparently was responsible for later reports by Nancy Shulins of the Associated Press and Nancy Kruh of the *Dallas Morning News*. The latter story was distributed by Knight–Ridder News Service.

Rajan reported to us that he had given 100 interviews as of March of 1990. Those included interviews with the *Kansas City Star, Miami Herald, Los Angeles Times, Denver Post, Calcutta Telegraph*, and *Times of India*. He was interviewed by *Discover, Omni*, and *People* magazines (but only the *People* interview led to an article). He had several radio and television interviews including "National Public Radio," "NBC Sunday Morning," "CBS News Nightwatch," "Larry King Live," the "Voice of America," "Republica TV of Italy," and the Australian version of "60 Minutes." In the first summer, the interviewing schedule became so intense that Rajan told us that he wanted to stop all interviews for a period of 6 months. We attempted to honor his request and refused interviews for him. However, after about 6 weeks, Rajan began to miss the action and began doing interviews again.

Rajan's intensive interview schedule gained him some local fame. The evidence of his popularity that was most satisfying to him was when he received a letter from Alexandria, Virginia addressed in a very unusual manner: The front of the letter contained a newspaper photo of Rajan with *Kansas State University, Manhattan, Kansas*, written below the photo. The post office sent the letter to the Department of Psychology without delay.

Rajan's performance during interviews was interesting to observe for those of us who were testing him. He was always entertaining and always gave demonstrations that dazzled the audience. At the same time, we had collected some laboratory data we could use to evaluate his responses to questions. We found that Rajan could no more resist the temptation to stretch the truth on occasion than can the average fisherman. We were always a bit surprised when he did this because Rajan's performance is startling without any exaggeration.

His exaggerations were typically modest, but occasionally, he told a whopper. His greatest "stretch," given to a naive TV audience, was in response to a question about how long it had taken him to learn the 35,000 digits of pi. Rajan responded that he learned 5,000 digits a day for a week and then took about 3 days to piece the parts together. We had data to show that his answer was a healthy exaggeration. Furthermore, Rajan notes in his autobiography that he had at least 10,000 digits mastered about 9 months prior to his performance. Taking that information in conjunction with our laboratory data, we are relatively certain that Rajan worked on memorizing the first 35,000 digits of pi for a minimum of a year.

The "Larry King Show"

Rajan is almost as skilled in doing interviews as he is at learning strings of digits. He is a naturally charming person who combines that charm with a great ability to tell stories and a willingness to display his talents. Consequently, talk show hosts are delighted to have him on their programs.

There was one occasion when Rajan's smooth and charming presentation covered a series of behind-the-scenes disasters that are hilarious only in retrospect. The interview was on the "Larry King Live" show on July 3, 1989. In typical fashion, the interview went smoothly, and Larry King went out of his way to compliment Rajan after the show. We are not sure that King knew of the events preceding the show, and he surely did not know what followed.

The problems began the night before the show. Throughout his stay at Kansas State, Rajan kept irregular and unusual hours. He was understandably excited about his scheduled appearance on the Larry King show, and he apparently spent a sleepless night pacing about his office and working in the animal research space. Two descriptive points are important for the story that follows: First, Rajan's clothes had been considerably soiled as a result of his work in the animal lab. Second, he had the ticket for the plane ride to Washington in his pocket.

About three in the morning, he left the building and walked to Manhattan (Kansas) city park, which is less than a half-mile away. After pacing about the park for a short time, he went into a restroom to use the facilities. As he entered, he slammed the door shut. When he went to leave, he found that he had jammed the door and couldn't get it open. The door was jammed, not locked, but Rajan is a slender man and he didn't have the strength to pull it open. Rajan cried out for help but, of course, no one was about at that time of night to hear his cries. Time passed slowly but inexorably. Minutes and hours rolled by as Rajan became more and more desperate to escape. After about 5 hours had passed, a security guard strolling around the park heard his cries and helped him open the door. Rajan was not wearing a watch and asked the guard for the time. Upon hearing the time, Rajan realized that he had only about 20 minutes to get to the airport and catch the plane. Fortunately, the airport is only about 10 minutes from the park, and Rajan was able to persuade the guard to give him a ride to the airport. He caught the plane from Manhattan with only the plane ticket and $5 in his pocket. To make matters worse, he was wearing terribly soiled clothes.

The producers of the show had someone waiting at the Washington airport to meet Rajan. Rajan explained that he had two problems: He didn't have any decent clothes to wear for the interview, and he had no money to buy his meals while in Washington. The producers solved the first problem by giving him $50 and instructing him to buy a shirt. They said that they would guarantee that the cameras would only focus on his face and chest so that viewers would be unaware of his soiled trousers. To solve the second problem, Rajan was instructed to take all his meals at the hotel so that the bill could be charged directly to the show. As we indicated earlier, the show went off beautifully, but Rajan had not yet reached the end of his misfortunes.

Rajan's return flight left Washington in early afternoon, so he slept in until 9 or 10 in the morning. After a leisurely shower, Rajan went down to the dining room for an equally leisurely and comfortable breakfast. Upon his return to his room, Rajan found that disaster had struck once more—his airline ticket was gone!

Rajan called an assistant manager and explained his plight. The assistant manager contacted the maintenance staff on the floor and talked to the maid responsible for the room. The maid stated that she had entered Rajan's room and saw no luggage. (Recall the circumstances of his departure from Manhattan meant that Rajan was traveling rather lightly.) She reasonably concluded the occupant had left the room. The airline ticket lying on the desk was treated as a bit of trash and thrown away!

Rajan and the assistant manager went to the basement and spent the better part of an hour sorting through the huge trash bins there. Eventually, they found the ticket and Rajan caught his plane back to the "Little Apple." We suspect that the circumstances surrounding Rajan's appearance on the Larry King show were somewhat more traumatic than most.

An Outrageous Interview

Rajan was always courteous and charming during his interviews. Unfortunately, the same cannot be said for all of the people who interviewed him.

Perhaps the most outrageous case of a nasty interviewer took place in the Psychology Department office at the beginning of a semester. The secretaries were fielding the usual flood of calls to the faculty that come early in a semester when they got a call from Chicago—"Can I speak to Rajan Mahadevan?"

Rajan was in the office getting a cup of coffee. This was not unusual because he consumed large amounts of coffee. He answered the phone to hear,

"This is a radio morning talk show from Chicago."
"A talk show?" Rajan replied quizzically.
"Yes. We're live."
"I'm on the air?" Rajan asked.

Of course, secretaries, faculty, and graduate students stopped whatever they were doing to eavesdrop. They are only human, after all.

"Are you the memory expert?"
"Yes."
"Well, we'd like to find out just how good you are. We'd like to give you a list of, say, 20 digits and see if you can repeat them back to us."
"Well," Rajan began, only to be interrupted by:
"We'd like to give you 20 digits, 5 digits per second."

Rajan tried to explain that the usual procedure for tests of memory span was to present the digits at one per second and that five per second was an unreasonable rate of presentation. The response by the talk show host was extremely rude, essentially suggesting that Rajan would either perform his test or be designated a fraud.

It was the only time we ever saw Rajan become furious with an interviewer. He slammed the headset into its cradle and stomped to his office. It was a rare instance when Rajan was glad *not* to show his prowess. In our view, his actions in response to the interviewer were totally justified.

Performing Before Professionals

Rajan captivated professional audiences as readily as lay audiences. We gave joint presentations to the Midwestern Psychological Association, the Psychonomic Society, and the European Society for Cognitive Psychology. In addition, we gave research colloquia at several universities. In these joint presentations, we would spend 30 to 45 minutes summarizing our research with Rajan, and then Rajan would give a 15- or 20-minute demonstration of his prowess. In every case, he was an outstanding success.

One of his most impressive performances was at the colloquium presented at the University of Kansas. As part of the presentation, members of the audience were given a sheet containing the first 5,000 digits of pi. The sheet is reproduced as Fig. 5.1. As shown in the figure, the digits were arranged in rows of 100 digits with five blocks of 10 rows each (i.e., 1,000 digits). We had arranged for someone (we'll call him Dan) to prepare an overhead that showed a target location (e.g., 4,367) along with the digit of pi at that location. Dan had made a common counting error in locating the target digits: People forget that the first row contains the digits in Locations 1 to 100. Thus, they assume that the digit at, for example, Location 3,701 is the first digit in row 37 when, in fact, it is the first digit in row 38. Dan had made that error for each target digit. As each target location was shown, Rajan took long enough to locate the digit in memory so that members of the audience could locate the digit on their sheets. Each time Rajan announced the digit at the target location, Dan "corrected" him. In each case, Rajan's choice was confirmed to be correct by the audience. After three such attempts, we noted that the score was now "Dan 0, Rajan 3" and asked whether we should continue the contest. The audience responded with a resounding "No!"

We then went on to another demonstration—one of Rajan's favorites. The numbers on the sheet described previously are grouped in blocks of 10 digits. Members of the audience begin reading the first five digits of a 10-digit block located anywhere in the first 5,000 digits of pi. Typically, before they finish reading the first five digits of the block, Rajan can continue by reciting the rest of the 10-digit block. After several successful attempts at this task, someone read a sequence rather slowly, and Rajan announced immediately "That sequence appears nowhere in the first 5,000 digits of pi!" The reader confessed that he had read down a column on the sheet of digits. The audience was astounded and very impressed by Rajan's ability. To know that a number sequence is in the set of digits of pi is one thing; to know it is not is quite another. Rajan later confessed to us that he was able to identify the ruse because pi does not repeat, and it happened that the sequence produced occurred as the beginning of a block in the second 5,000 digits of pi. We found it equally impressive that Rajan, completely unprepared for a string of digits from the second 5,000, could recognize one so rapidly.

Rajan's performance before the European Society for Cognitive Psychology is worth noting because it illustrates that interest in Rajan was widespread. The presentation was a success as usual. Charles Thompson stated the outcome with resigned amusement in a postcard to his colleagues, "They listened to me with extreme politeness. Then they threw rose petals in Rajan's path as he strode to and from the speaker's platform." Thompson has provided the following description of an event connecting Rajan to the famous memorist Shereshevskii (S) who was described in detail by the Russian psychologist Luria.

> The day after our presentation, while waiting for the noon talk to begin, an individual sitting behind me introduced himself. He said he was from the University of Moscow and gave me his name but I didn't quite catch it (a search of the program suggests it must have been B. Velichkovsky). He said he had been with Luria during a portion of the time when Luria was working on his book, *The Mind of a Mnemonist*. He thanked us for our presentation and said he greatly enjoyed it because it brought memories of that time with Luria flooding back. I was very interested in hearing about his experience with Luria, but the talk began before I could pursue the conversation further. When I turned to resume the conversation after the presentation, Velichkovsky was gone and I did not see him again.

TYPICAL QUESTIONS TO RAJAN

No matter who constituted the audience when Rajan performed, he was always asked a series of questions that were quite predictable. What follows is a reconstruction of a typical set of questions together with the usual content of his answers. Depending on the situation, he might make a joke of the answer or shrug it off. Whatever style he adopted, he was almost always charming and effective.

Some of the questions were interesting in that they could only be answered correctly with a controlled comparison of specific learning conditions. Because Rajan did not have such data, he would reply based on what seemed reasonable to him. Our experiments have provided data to correct Rajan's answers. Thus, in the following section, we comment on his responses when it seems appropriate. As we comment, keep in mind that Rajan did not have the information from controlled experiments available as he developed his answers over the course of his life. Indeed, even though he now has those data available, it may be difficult for him to change some of his very effective answers.

"When did you discover that you had this talent?"

Rajan's parents had a large party for his sister on the occasion of her first birthday. He was 5 years old at the time. As noted in his autobiography, he memorized the license plates of the cars in the parking lot and recited them to the guests. He was able to pair each license plate with an appropriate guest, which impressed the group considerably. Rajan indicated that it was the first time that he realized he was "fairly good at remembering numbers." Rajan's father confirmed this story in a letter to us.

"Is your ability mostly inherited or mostly learned?"

Rajan said he suspected that there is a genetic component to his ability. His father learned large portions of Shakespeare and claims to have memorized enormous amounts of material while in medical school. His brother also is quite good at memorizing names and faces.

"What prompted you to learn 35,000 digits of pi?"

He often stated that several friends had challenged him to do something special to show that he was particularly good at remembering numbers. It seemed to him that learning enough digits to enter the *Guinness Book of World Records* would be good evidence of his ability. The challenge prompted him to set about the task, and he succeeded.

"How long did it take you to learn the 35,000 digits?"

His answer to this question varied a great deal, but he usually implied that he did it rather quickly. Typically, the time span given was a few weeks or a few months. He invariably stated with good humor that the hardest job was getting "victims" to listen to his recitations to ensure that he had the sequence learned correctly.

There are no records of his efforts but, as we stated earlier, we think that he spent over a year on the task. We are fairly confident that he attacked the digits in blocks of 1,000 because that was his strategy on his occasional attempts to learn extra digits of pi. Our data suggest that although it would not be difficult for him to master reciting a block of 1,000 in a day, it would take more time for him to become confident of that recitation. We speculate that it took him about a week to master 1,000 digits with confidence. In addition, he would need several weeks to piece the blocks into one long sequence.

"Do you intend to learn more digits of pi?"

Rajan usually stated with great confidence that he intended to increase his memorized sequence to 100,000 digits of pi. While he was at Kansas State University, he occasionally did try to learn additional digits, but those attempts came in spurts and did not last long. Barring some substantial incentive, we do not think that Rajan will improve his 1981 performance.

Our speculation is based primarily on our experience when we began testing Rajan on a portion of the digits he had previously learned. The last portion of this book reports rather extensive tests performed on Rajan's retrieval from memory of the first 10,000 digits of pi. We had intended to perform those tests on the first 20,000 digits of pi, but Rajan resisted that attempt. He was very nervous when we began the tests, so we gave him the opportunity to practice reciting the digits as a way to reassure him of his ability to perform. We spent about 2 weeks (at 2 hours per day) reviewing the first 10,000 digits at the rate of about 1,000 digits per day.

Once we completed 10,000 digits, Rajan resisted going any further. We spent 3 or 4 days covering only about 500 digits. His resistance was obvious because we previously had established that Rajan could learn a 20 × 20 matrix (400 digits) in about 35 minutes. We concluded that Rajan did not want to be tested on more than the first 10,000 digits of pi. It may be that he only wanted to be tested on the digits with which he was extremely familiar. We came to believe that he would need additional practice on the digits between 10,000 and 35,000 before he went on to learn additional digits.

"How do you learn a large matrix of numbers?"

Rajan said that he just fixated on each number for a few seconds until he "knew" he had it and then went on to the next number. When pressed for a more illuminating response, he said that being asked to describe how he learned numbers was like being asked to describe how he rode a bicycle. He knew how to do both tasks, but he found it difficult to describe either process.

Rajan's response expressed some frustration and, from what is known of skilled performance, was perfectly accurate. That is, as performance becomes more and more skilled, it also becomes less and less available to conscious inspection. It was not at all surprising that Rajan's skilled performance had become automatic and unavailable to him.

"Do you have a mental image of the matrices you learn?"

Rajan denied having any sort of photographic memory. He would describe in detail the manner in which he learned a matrix of numbers. He learned each row as a unit and learned the first column as a marker for the rows. Our research (see chapter 4) showed that his description was accurate. Further, if Rajan had a strong visual image, he would be able to read either a row or a column from that image with equal ease. Our research showed that he could give any row of a matrix with ease, but it took considerable effort for him to reconstruct a column of the matrix. In addition, our tests (see chapter 3) suggested that his imagery was certainly not above, and was possibly below, average.

"How long do you remember a number matrix?"

Rajan replied that his memory for a matrix was rather variable, ranging from rapid forgetting to memory for many years. We were able to verify that he had retained the first four matrices from the Minnesota tests when he was tested almost 9 years later. Of course, we have no information on how often he might have practiced those matrices; however, we are fairly confident that he did not record them. We also have evidence that some matrices were forgotten in a matter of days (see chapter 4).

"What else can you do with your ability?"

In answering this question, Rajan usually cited examples of learning phone numbers and street addresses. He often suggested that he could make a "killing" at Las Vegas. We never tested his ability to count cards, but we think he could have developed that ability rather quickly. He did have a large number of phone numbers and street addresses readily available. On one occasion, we were planning a trip, and Rajan offered to give us the "800" numbers for various airlines. He gave us about a dozen "800" numbers for airlines and offered to give us many more. We checked about eight or nine of the numbers; they were completely accurate.

The numbers he remembered were often arcane. During a test of his memory span, he told Thad Cowan, "Those four numbers are the year you were tenured." He was correct.

"Does this ability extend to areas other than numbers?"

Rajan usually claimed or implied that his memorizing ability was quite general. To the contrary, our research strongly suggested that, with the exception of performance on letter span, his memorizing ability did not differ in any substantial way from that of an ordinary college student. The implications of our research were confirmed by additional studies by Alan Baddeley (Baddeley, Mahadevan, & Thompson, 1992).

"Does this ability help you in your classes?"

Rajan usually said that his ability helped him with his classwork. That answer is very interesting because it probably is true for reasons other than those that Rajan thought were operating. To people who taught Rajan in classes, it appeared that he attempted to memorize material from both text and lecture notes in much the same manner as he had memorized large strings of numbers.

The data on Rajan's performance suggests that his memorization strategy probably was not optimal because his memorizing ability on material other than digits was no better or no worse than an average college student's. However, we speculate that Rajan's belief that he could memorize large amounts of material was an important motivator when he studied. In short, although his strategy was not optimal, his motivation was high, and he undoubtedly learned a great deal as a result.

RAJAN AS A PERSON

Rajan as a Student

People frequently ask us about Rajan as a student. In particular, they want to know if his memory skills helped him on tests.

It is fair to say that Rajan was an average to above-average graduate student in class. He did not always read the assignments when given, and he would try to cram for examinations. Rajan had a tendency to try to commit the reading assignments to memory and reproduce them on tests. The strategy of giving back information on tests sometimes works in undergraduate courses, but it is counterproductive in graduate courses where students are asked to apply their knowledge and understanding to new situations.

When taking tests, Rajan would write furiously for the entire test period. Frequently he was the last one to finish, and he always wrote far more than everyone else. His examinations contained page upon page of paraphrase from the reading assignments. He did not reproduce the text exactly or even always accurately. His strategy appeared to be to write as much as he could remember in hopes that the correct answer was somewhere in his response. His handwriting was sloppy, and he would go back and make insertions which made his answers quite difficult to read.

On more than one occasion, Rajan said that he stayed up all night to study. When he did this, he looked more disheveled than usual. His erratic lifestyle tended to catch up with him when he tried to cram in this manner.

In quantitative classes, Rajan tried to impress everyone with his skill as a mental calculator. On many occasions, data were generated on the spot and the calculations were done on the board as a class effort. Rajan confessed to one of us that he committed to memory a number of algorithms for rapid calculation; however, he tended to be incorrect when he tried to do a multiplication or division in his head.

Despite his disorganized lifestyle and tendency to try to memorize everything he read, Rajan was still an average to above-average student. Sometimes his answers contained evidence of interesting insights. As he progressed in our graduate program, he tended to rely less on the strategy of memorizing everything and more on trying to understand and organize the information. He also became more reliable in attending class and keeping appointments.

Rajan earned a Master's degree in cognitive psychology from Kansas State University in the summer of 1991. He entered the University of Colorado in the fall of 1991 to continue his graduate studies in cognitive psychology.

Rajan as a Subject

Despite the fact that Rajan enjoyed being the star performer on our research project, he enjoyed even more the opportunity to impress others. During the second year of the project, Rajan cracked a rib when he slipped and fell in the bathtub. He kept an appointment to perform in front of a general psychology class the next morning even though he was obviously in pain. However, being tested by us was a different matter; Rajan did not come to any of our twice-a-day scheduled test sessions for the next 3 weeks.

At the beginning of the project, Rajan was tested by our paid assistants. He balked at this arrangement and let it be known that he wanted to be tested by us. This was both a blessing and a curse. Although it put us in close contact with him on a daily basis and allowed us the opportunity to make casual observations that sometimes became the source of new experiments, it was an endless source of frustration.

Rajan missed scheduled test sessions on many occasions. After the first year, we reached an agreement—we would warn him when he was missing too many sessions and, if he continued to miss sessions, we would dock him a month's pay. That procedure was helpful, but twice during the remaining months of the project we had to dock him a month's pay for missed sessions. He also had the annoying habit of being chronically late for the test sessions. As exasperating as this was to us, he compounded our frustration by never waiting if we were late or were not in the test room when he arrived. He shaped us well; we adopted the strategy of bringing reading materials so that we could wait for him to arrive.

Although some of his actions were annoying, Rajan made many positive contributions to our research. He was intensely interested in his memory and made many insightful comments that led either to the addition of conditions in experiments or to new experiments. He was a true collaborator as well as a subject in the research on his memory. As a result, he earned his place on a major publication as well as on several paper presentations.

Reciting pi

This chapter would be incomplete without a description of Rajan's recitation of 31,811 decimal digits of pi without error. He is justifiably proud of that feat. The performance clearly established that he has an exceptionally trained memory for digits and put him firmly in the ranks of world class memorists.

The *Guinness Book of World Records* required that two invigilators, together with two witnesses, view and certify his performance. The invigilators kept records of the time to recite each block of 1,000 digits and the duration of all breaks. We have examined those records and find that Rajan recited the 31,811 digits in 150 minutes (not including 75 minutes of rest breaks). The statement in the

Guinness Book of World Records, for reasons we do not understand, says he only took 26 minutes for rest breaks and extends his overall time by 4 minutes. Based on the records of the invigilators, his overall rate of presentation was a very rapid 3.5 digits per second. His rate for the initial 10,000 digits was a breathtaking 4.9 digits per second. An important implication of Rajan's very rapid rate of presentation is that he could not have been using a mnemonic (i.e., a system for storing and recalling items) to remember the digits. His presentation rate precluded the necessary time for retrieval and interpretation of a mnemonic.

Rajan was replaced in the *Guinness Book of World Records* by Hideaki Tomoyori who recited 40,000 digits on March 9, 1987. The contrast between the two memorists is interesting. Tomoyori took 786 minutes (excluding 255 minutes of rest breaks) to recite the 40,000 digits. His presentation rate was .85 digits per second. Rajan stated that Tomoyori used a *story mnemonic* based on the second meaning that all words for single digits have in Japanese. Thus, Tomoyori was able to weave those words into a long story mnemonic that he used to retrieve the 40,000 digits. The time necessary to retrieve the story mnemonic presumably produced his rather slow recitation rate of less than one digit per second.

It is an open question as to which memorist gave the more impressive performance. As will become clear later in the book, Rajan uses a rather intellectually barren procedure to learn and retrieve digit strings. Put differently, he seems to rely on raw memory power. For that reason, we tend to think that Rajan's rapid retrieval of almost 32,000 digits was more impressive than Tomoyori's slower retrieval of 40,000 digits.

There is an interesting addendum to Rajan's mastery of pi. He often recites the first one or two thousand digits of pi as a demonstration. He can now present those digits at an incredible rate approaching seven digits per second. Many readers find it impossible to follow Rajan on a printed page of digits when he recites at that rate. We discovered an interesting perceptual effect for those unable to follow Rajan. If the listener jumps ahead 100 or 200 digits and focuses on a series of 4 or 5 digits, the listener will hear Rajan recite that series as he speeds past that location. It tends to be a somewhat startling perceptual effect.

Rajan's Sense of Humor

We close this chapter with an example of Rajan's well-developed sense of humor. His humor is a bit difficult to capture in writing because it is subtle, somewhat mischievous, and is best appreciated when accompanied by Rajan's captivating grin and the impish twinkle in his eyes. The following account by Stephen Kiefer (with whom Rajan worked in the physiological lab) captures a bit of Rajan's humor.

At the end of the semester, I typically take the students working in my lab out to lunch as a way of rewarding them for their hard work. In this particular instance, there were about three graduate students [Rajan included] and maybe one undergraduate. We went to one of the local eateries. At the end of the meal, I paid the tab with a charge card, as I typically do. I'm not certain how it came up but, on the way out of the restaurant, we were talking about charge cards, dollar limits, etc. Someone jokingly asked Rajan if he had his card number memorized and he remarked that, no, he didn't. But he did have my number memorized and proceeded to rattle it off at his usual 5-6 digits per second, all with this mischievous smile on his face. I checked and indeed he had looked at my card somehow and had committed the card number to memory. I told him that if some mysterious charges started showing up on my bill, I'd know where they came from! (Incidentally, I closed my account not too long after that; although I seem to recall that the closure was for a good reason, it may have been because I knew, deep down, that my number was floating around out there.)

Stephen Kiefer's story portrays a typical Rajan prank. He made good use of his memory skill to amuse himself (and us) in a mischievous way. It portrays that which we liked most about Rajan — he was friendly, fun-loving, and had a good sense for what constituted a harmless joke. We remember him fondly.

Memory Span and Memory Load Tasks

The next three chapters focus on a series of tests which, taken together, give an overall view of Rajan's abilities. Although there is much new material in these chapters, many of these tests also have been described by Thompson, Cowan, Frieman, Mahadevan, Vogl, and Frieman (1991).

In addition to describing Rajan's abilities, we relate his performance to the theory of skilled memory developed by Chase and Ericsson (e.g., Chase & Ericsson, 1981, 1982). They proposed three general principles for skilled memory and illustrated these principles with subjects having particular expertise (e.g., Ericsson & Polson, 1988). These three principles are meaningful encoding (the use of preexisting knowledge to encode the presented information), retrieval structure (explicitly attaching retrieval cues to the encoded material to allow efficient retrieval) and speed-up (a reduction in study time with further practice).

Based on their research, Chase and Ericsson conclude that the skilled memory shown by memorists can be achieved by any normal subject. More recently, Ericsson and Faivre (1988) argued that there is no available evidence that exceptional abilities, including exceptional memory, represent anything other than extensive practice effects. They state that their studies showing "remarkable improvement in 'basic' processes raises serious doubt regarding the validity of the assumption of inherited basic aptitudes" (p. 467).

We report a series of tests on Rajan showing that his performance demonstrates two of the general principles proposed by Chase and Ericsson (*retrieval structure* and *speed-up*). However, his encoding procedure does not appear to be consistent with the third principle (*meaningful encoding*). Chase and Ericsson suggest that, in the absence of such encoding, a normal subject will show a memory span of about seven items. We present evidence that Rajan did not use these coding techniques and still produced spans of 60 or more digits. We propose that Rajan's performance represents a combination of extensive practice and above-normal ability.

Finally, we end this chapter with a report of some surprising performance by our control subjects in a parallel processing task. These data have, we think, important implications for a portion of the working memory model (e.g., Baddeley, 1992; Baddeley & Hitch, 1974).

MEMORY SPAN

The formal tests on Rajan began with a measure of his memory span. As noted earlier, memory span is a measure of the number of digits that can be correctly repeated in order when the digits are presented at a rate of one per second. It is one of the standard measures of memory ability. When measured on normal individuals without practice at the task, it is extremely rare to find memory spans less than 4 digits or greater than 11 digits. To the best of our knowledge, Rajan was first exposed to a memory span test in 1980 when he was tested at the University of Minnesota (Hanson, 1980; Horn, 1981). His digit span was 15, well above the normal range when the material was presented auditorially.

It appeared that Rajan's memory span had increased substantially in the following 8 years because our informal tests suggested that his digit span was around 40. This increase was not surprising, given Chase and Ericsson's reports that people with ordinary ability can develop long digit spans after considerable practice (Chase & Ericsson, 1981, 1982; Ericsson, 1985, 1988; Ericsson & Chase, 1982; Ericsson, Chase, & Faloon, 1980; Ericsson & Faivre, 1988). Ericsson and his colleagues showed data from subjects who developed digits spans over 80 digits with the use of mnemonics and extensive practice. Rajan enjoys tasks involving numbers; therefore, it seems highly probable that he would have practiced the memory span task once he discovered it.

Rajan's memory span posed three separate problems. First, it was necessary to obtain a current measure of his span. Next, it was necessary to establish that his span would increase with practice. That would lend credence to our speculation that his increase in span (following the initial tests) was attributable to practice. Further, if his span did increase with practice, the rate of increase was of some interest. Given Rajan's skill with numbers, it seemed quite possible that he also might develop the skill necessary to increase his span very rapidly. Finally, the most difficult challenge was to estimate what his memory span was prior to practice on the memory span task. We refer to his memory span prior to practice as his baseline memory span.

Current Memory Span

In the memory span tests (and many other tests), Rajan's performance was compared to the performance of control subjects. Because Rajan had so much experience working with numbers, we attempted to get control subjects who would also become quite experienced working with digits. Thus, we hired control subjects who would be likely to continue through the 3 years of the project studying Rajan. We selected two male and two female undergraduate students at Kansas State University. They were chosen on the basis of a good grade point average (3.0 or better on a 4.0 scale), class standing (first or second year), and normal memory span (6-9 digits). The selection criteria worked reasonably well as three of the control subjects stayed for the entire duration of the project; the fourth stayed for 2 of the 3 years.

The control subjects and Rajan were tested on both letter span and digit span. Each type of span was measured using both auditory and visual presentation. The initial letter span tests used vowels and consonants. To reduce the possibility of pronounceable sequences, we repeated the letter span tests with only consonants and found that letter span had not changed.

A computer was used to generate a random series for each span. Prior to presentation, each series was printed so that the experimenter could verify recall and, in the case of auditory presentation, present the series. The letters or digits either appeared in the center of the computer monitor or were spoken by the experimenter. The items appeared on the screen, or were spoken, one at a time at a rate of one per second. To avoid visual masking, the items appeared for .75 second, with a .25 second blank period between the numbers. The subjects were given 50 trials with the length of the series set at seven items for the first trial. When the subject correctly repeated the series, the length was increased by one item. When the subject made an error, the length was decreased by one item. Memory span was defined as the mean sequence length for the last 10 trials of the 50-trial series.

Letter Span.   Rajan's memory span of 13 letters was the same for visual and auditory presentation. For comparison, the memory spans for the four control subjects ranged from six to nine letters with a mean of seven letters. Like Rajan, their mean span was identical for both visual and auditory presentation.

Digit Span.   Unlike letter span, Rajan's memory span differed dramatically for visual and auditory presentation. His auditory digit span was 43 whereas his visual digit span was 28. The control subjects produced a memory span of 7 digits (with a range of 6 to 9) under auditory presentation and a span of 8 digits (with a range of 7 to 9) under visual presentation. Their performance was quite consistent with the data from a classic study by Gates (1916) in which college students showed a digit memory span of 7.7 with auditory presentation and 8.2 with visual presentation.

Rajan believes that he does much better with auditory presentation than with visual presentation, and the observed difference appears to support his view. However, he was having some health problems when he was tested on visual digit span. It seemed to us that the difference might be attributed to either health or motivation produced by his belief that he was better at auditory presentation. About a year later, Rajan had improved his visual memory span to about 60 digits. We reasoned that, if there were a modality difference attributable to something other than motivation or health, Rajan should be able to produce an auditory span in excess of 60 digits. He was not able to do so. Indeed, it took several days to bring his auditory span up to the level of his visual span. We have interpreted those data, taken together with the letter span data, to mean that Rajan shows no modality difference in memory span.

Practice on Memory Span

We speculated that Rajan's increase in memory span following the Minnesota tests was the result of practice. If that were true, he should show additional gains in span with additional practice. Thus, we gave Rajan and the control subjects additional practice on memory span to determine whether their span would increase. The control subjects were given 16 hours of additional practice (in hour or half-hour blocks) on digit span. Because Rajan was engaged in some additional tests during this period, he only accumulated 7 hours of practice. Only visual presentation was used during the practice sessions.

Increase in Memory Span.   The memory spans for all subjects increased. At the end of the 16 hours of practice, the visual memory spans for the control subjects (as measured by the mean of the last 10 trials) ranged from 9 to 12 digits.

Rajan's memory span increased at a more rapid rate than the control subjects. His visual memory span had increased to 37 digits after 7 hours of practice. Plotting performance in hour blocks, Rajan's rate of gain as measured by the slope of the function was 1.19. By contrast, the slopes for the controls ranged from .08 to .27.

We noted earlier that Ericsson and his colleagues had trained subjects to very high spans. Our two best control subjects compared favorably with Chase and Ericsson's (1982) two successful subjects. We estimated the slopes for those two subjects, DD and SF, to be .22 and .32, respectively.

Baseline Span and Improvement with Practice.   The University of Minnesota tests were Rajan's first encounter with the memory span procedure. Our tests showed that Rajan's digit span had increased substantially over the 8-year period since that first test. However, his increase in digit span did not appear to be accompanied by an increase in letter span. That outcome was consistent with the results of Ericsson, Chase, and Faloon (1980) demonstrating that their memory expert (SF) showed no transfer of his much improved digit span to a letter span test. As we noted, additional practice on digit span raised Rajan's visual digit span to almost 60. We retested Rajan's letter span at that point and found it to be 12, which essentially is indistinguishable from our initial measurement of 13 letters. It would appear that practice increased Rajan's digit span and, as with the Ericsson et al. (1980) results, the practice which successfully increased digit span had no effect on letter span.

Span Length and Rehearsal Time

In our initial measures of memory span, there was a marked difference between the control subjects and Rajan in repeating the span. The control subjects usually repeated the string as soon as the signal to repeat the string was given. Rajan usually paused for some time before he repeated the series of digits.

We hypothesized that Rajan had increased his digit span by systematically encoding subsequences of the span. Before responding, he would have to rehearse those short sequences and ensure that they were strung together in the right order. In other words, subjects who have developed encoding procedures to master long sequences would have to spend some time decoding the sequence to ensure accuracy. If our speculations were correct, recall of a sequence should be immediate until the sequence becomes supraspan. At that point, rehearsal of the encoded sequence would produce a delay in recall. Further increases in sequence length should produce a greater delay in recall. The sequence length at which a subject begins to delay recall should mark the transition from span to supraspan sequences. It seemed a promising possibility as a method for estimating Rajan's baseline memory span. Thus, we tested our hypothesis in a experiment in which span length was systematically varied for each subject.

The memory span bounds for the control subjects in this experiment were set at two for the lower bound and one below their current span for the upper bound. The lower bound for Rajan was set at 5 digits and the upper bound was set at 30 digits.

In any session, subjects were given either an ascending series or a descending series. In an ascending series, subjects started at a lower bound, with span increasing by one following an errorless recall until the upper bound was reached. In a descending series, they started at the upper bound, and the span was decreased by one following an errorless recall until the lower bound was reached. All subjects were given 20 ascending and 20 descending series.

We added one control subject for this experiment. One of our testers (DW) became quite fascinated with the strategies and performance of the control subjects. He developed a memory span task on his home computer and practiced intensively over one weekend. He announced with pride on Monday morning that he was able to produce a span over 20. We gave him 50 trials using visual presentation with the other conditions the same as the initial trials for our controls. His mean performance on the last 10 trials was 22 digits. As a result of training, the memory spans for the other control subjects now ranged from 10 to 17.

Rehearsal Time.   The critical measure in this experiment was rehearsal time, which was defined as the time between the end of the sequence (marked with an asterisk on the computer screen) and the beginning of the recitation of the sequence. The rehearsal time data were tabulated separately for ascending and descending series, and only the rehearsal times for correct span production were considered. The median rehearsal time for each subject was plotted for each length. The data for Rajan, GN, and DW are shown in Figs. 2.1, 2.2, and 2.3, respectively.

For those three subjects, rehearsal times remained quite low up to a certain span length, which differed for each subject. At that point, rehearsal times increased rather rapidly. We propose that this point of inflection should provide a reasonable approximation of memory span prior to practice. These data are consistent with our hypothesis. The break point for GN is nine, and his memory span was originally measured at seven. We have no initial measure of DW's span, but the inflection at about eight is within the normal range of memory spans.

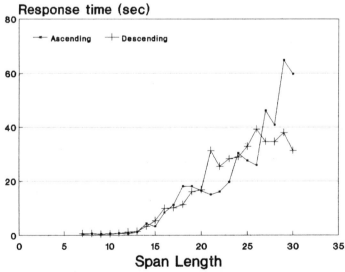

FIG. 2.1.   Median rehearsal times for each memory span length. The data are from Rajan and are presented separately for ascending and descending series. Reprinted from Thompson, C. P., Cowan, T. M., Frieman, J., Mahadevan, R. S., Vogl, R. J., & Frieman, J. (1991). Rajan: A study of a memorist. *Journal of Memory and Language, 30,* 702–724, with permission of Academic Press.

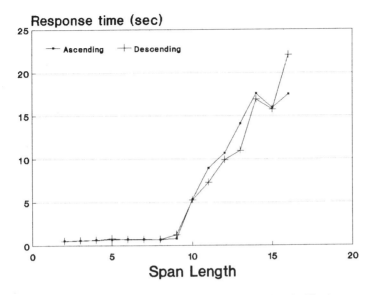

FIG. 2.2. Median rehearsal times for each memory span length. The data are from GN and are presented separately for ascending and descending series. Reprinted from Thompson et al. (1991), with permission.

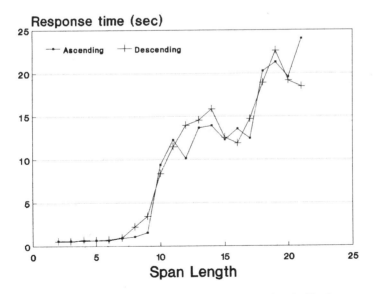

FIG. 2.3. Median rehearsal times for each memory span length. The data are from DW and are presented separately for ascending and descending series. Reprinted from Thompson et al. (1991), with permission.

Most importantly, Rajan's break point is conservatively estimated to be length 13, and his span was originally measured at 15. Thus, these data lend support to the hypothesis that his baseline memory span was in the 13 to 15 digit range.

We note here that it is common to observe an hysteresis effect when ascending and descending series are used in psychophysical experiments. No hysteresis was observed in this experiment.

Three of our subjects (MD, TH, and DA) showed no change in rehearsal time; MD and TH had only increased their memory spans two or three digits above their baseline. Thus, there was little room to demonstrate an inflection in their rehearsal time, and the failure to do so should not be surprising. However, DA provides a more troublesome exception to what otherwise can be interpreted as a rather clear set of data. DA had increased his memory span from 8 to 13. He was, therefore, tested on span lengths ranging from 2 to 12. Thus, we expected to see an increase in rehearsal time starting about length 8 but his rehearsal times remained at about .6 seconds over the entire range. We must conclude that the ascending–descending procedure is not decisively analytic. However, we believe the data are strongly suggestive of baseline performance when a break point is observed.

We note that digit spans are typically about one item larger than letter spans (e.g., Brener, 1940). Thus, the original Minnesota tests, our tests of letter span, and the rehearsal time data all suggest that Rajan's digit span prior to practice was between 12 and 15 digits.

Strategies for Encoding Memory Span

Control Subjects. We interviewed the control subjects at the end of the memory span tests and the strategies they reported using are noted here. All of the subjects developed strategies for encoding the digits. Three of the subjects (GN, DA, and DW) developed very effective strategies to increase their memory span, and two (MD and TH) did not. The critical difference appeared to be that the unsuccessful subjects changed their encoding strategy with each sequence. TH chunked the digits into groups of three or four depending on the composition of the presented sequence and the length of the sequence. MD looked for encodable chunks in the string and varied her encoding strategy accordingly. Interestingly, in addition to their subjects who reached memory spans exceeding 80 digits, Chase and Ericsson (1981) reported a subject who reached asymptotic performance at a length of 18 digits. Like our subjects, that subject used a strategy of grouping digits during presentation. This was in contrast to their other subjects (and our other control subjects) who used a predetermined method for chunking the digits. The data from both laboratories are consistent in showing that a chunking strategy based on the presented sequence is not very effective. We speculate that two factors contribute to the failure of the postpresentation approach relative to a procedure for chunking digit strings which has been set prior to presentation of the series. First, the relatively rapid rate of presentation in a memory span task undoubtedly makes it difficult to develop strategies as the digits are appearing. Second, a stable chunking scheme has the dual benefit of providing a standard procedure for encoding and a standard procedure for retrieval. With a stable chunking scheme, the subject needs only to develop some procedures for handling strings that do not fit for one reason or another.

The successful encoding schemes developed by GN and DA were quite different. On each trial, DA decided to block the digits in groups of either three or four digits and then attempted to relate the groups to previous knowledge. To give a few examples, he remembered the string 357 as a gun, 454 as an engine size, and 173 as the room number of a particular lecture hall. His strategy was essentially the same as that adopted by Chase and Ericsson's successful subjects. In contrast, GN always blocked the digits in groups of four and attempted to relate the groups using mathematical principles. He divided the block of four into two pairs of digits and used mathematical relationships such as sums, multiples, and squares to relate both the pairs and the blocks of four. As a minor strategy, he related the digits to previous knowledge. For example, 46 was recalled as his high school football number. He was a student in engineering and his familiarity with mathematics may account for the rather unusual strategy.

Like our other two successful subjects, DW used an encoding scheme which was fixed prior to presentation of the series. He blocked the digits into groups of four and related the digit groups to either sports or money. The sports mnemonic consisted mainly of baseball, basketball, and golf information. The money mnemonic consisted of real and imagined salaries from his personal history. To reduce interference, DW cleverly alternated the two mnemonics on successive trials. He also changed the sport mnemonic from trial to trial by using, for example, golf information on one trial and basketball information on the next "sports trial."

Rajan.　　Rajan's procedure for encoding digit span appeared to be markedly different in two respects from the subjects achieving supraspan performance reported by Chase and Ericsson (e.g., 1981, 1982). First, Rajan stated that his group size varied from 14 to 17 digits, and he did not decide in advance how to group the digits. On that point, Rajan appeared to behave like the Chase and Ericsson (1981) subject whose performance reached asymptote at about 18 digits. Chase and Ericsson attributed her failure to attain a higher span to her strategy of grouping digits during presentation. Clearly, that strategy posed no problem for Rajan.

Second, Rajan always described a procedure for learning a memory span sequence which resembles paired-associate (or cue–target) learning. The correct digits are the targets and the cues are the location in the list. He stated that he kept track of the location of each digit while learning sequences of 14 to 17 digits. He then put together the shorter sequences to give the complete string.

It is significant that Rajan insisted on knowing the length of the sequence before it was presented for recall. One implication of this is that the location bins are set firmly into place prior to presentation. However, Rajan said that he is flexible about sequence length so that he can take advantages of patterns (e.g., 01010) that might occur at the end of a sequence. Assuming this is true, knowledge of length might set some maximum which can be shortened as he pleases. Without knowledge of length, he must add location bins as he goes; the location bin would be constructed *after* the appearance of the to-be-remembered item. The item would be adrift momentarily, an orphan seeking a home.

Rajan stated that he kept track of the location of each digit in the sequence (e.g., Location 33) and not the location in the shorter sequence (e.g., Location 3 in the third group of five). Our observations suggest that he learned shorter sequences ranging from 10 to 15 digits and kept track of the starting location of those sequences. However, he also had to rehearse the shorter sequences and often did a memory search for one or more specific digits within the sequence. For example, if he remembered all but 2 digits in a string of 15, he was able to hold the remembered digits in his mind while doing a serial search (i.e., 00, 01, 02, 03, etc.) for the missing digits.

Although we have no formal data on the point, we all observed Rajan engaging in a memory search while holding other digits in mind. Two characteristics of this behavior are intriguing: First, he did not seem to have any trouble holding the other digits in mind even when he dealt with spans of 40 or 50 digits. Second, he appeared to be able to recognize the missing digits when he did his serial search. Our impression is that this strategy usually succeeded, although it did fail occasionally.

Rajan said that, although he does not use chunking of three or four digits as a consistent strategy, his procedure sometimes includes such chunking. He stated that he takes advantage of sequences that he recognizes to "shorten the list." For example, he encodes a sequence of 865 as "1865—the year of Lincoln's death" and 111 as "a Nelson because Admiral Nelson had one eye, one arm, and one leg." (Rajan's examples are interesting but historically inaccurate—Nelson did not lose a leg!)

It is important to note that Rajan may not recognize an encodable sequence during presentation. We often observed Rajan recite a sequence and then state that he did not notice one or two encodable strings in the sequence until the recitation.

Chase and Ericsson (1981,1982) stressed that subjects achieve supraspan performance by grouping digits into chunks which can be tied to preexisting knowledge (encodable chunks). Our observations of Rajan in the memory span studies lead us to believe that, while encodable chunks occasionally help Rajan in learning a sequence, he did not require encodable chunks for learning or retrieving a sequence.

Regardless of what sort of retrieval structure is being used (encodable chunks or paired-associate sequences), deep encoding might be demonstrated in at least two ways. There should be evidence for long-term retention of the encoded chunk or sequence, and similar sequences could interfere with one another. Evidence from records taken during the ascending–descending memory span study shows both the predicted retention and interference effects. While this demonstrates the presence of deep encoding, it does not discriminate between the chunking hypothesis of Chase and Ericsson (1982) and the modified paired-associate strategy we propose for Rajan. However, the specific form which interference takes does discriminate between the two hypotheses.

Segments of previous trials sometimes interfere in a very specific way with his performance. To cite one example, Rajan failed to recall a sequence correctly in a series of ascending spans. He noted that the digits in positions 10, 11, and 12 were 904 in the current series whereas the digits in positions 10, 11, and 12 in a series four trials back were 903. He simply could not remember whether the 4 or the 3 belonged in this series. His memory for the digits and locations was entirely accurate.

This example is consistent with a system that encodes digits by location but is not consistent with a procedure that chunks the two sequences by relating them to preexisting knowledge. Under the latter procedure, the two strings would be coded as disparate events (e.g., 1903 is the year of the first flight by the Wright brothers, and 1904 is the year that B. F. Skinner was born), and neither of these should be confused with the other.

In the experiment using ascending and descending spans, we asked Rajan to recall any number segments he could remember following each of two sessions. He was not forewarned of either test. The two recalls included the three series (two ascending and one descending) presented in those two sessions. These data were pooled and only unique sequences from recall were used in our analysis. That is, we did not include any sequence which appeared more than once in the day's sessions. This excluded three single digits and three double digits, all of which appeared to be recalled in the correct location, and one triple digit sequence.

There were 28 remaining digit strings that Rajan uniquely recalled. Only one of these strings appeared nowhere in any of the spans presented during that session. (However, the first six digits of that string matched the start of a presented span and the other four digits may have occurred in a previous session.) Rajan identified the locations of 25 out of the 27 remaining unique sequences and was within one space for the other two.

We classified the 27 unique sequences into three types: (a) strings taken entirely from a span within the session and correctly located (22 cases), (b) strings taken entirely from a span within the session with location shifted by one space (2 cases), and (c) strings correctly located but taken in part from one span and in part from another span (3 cases). An example of each type of string is given in Table 2.1.

TABLE 2.1
Data Illustrating Accuracy of Location of Sequences in Final Recall for
Two Ascending (A) and One Descending (D) Memory Span Series

1. Accurate location of first digit in string. (22 cases)
   Presented span (A): 58730100917555361395
   Recall: 301009

2. One space error in locating first digit. (2 cases)
   Presented span (A): 84258717945917501
   Recall: 1750

3. Accurate location but string is from two spans. (3 cases)
   Presented span (A23): 28659034815720810018649
   Recall: 1572087547791
   Presented span (A22): 7094371319364127547791

   Rajan's performance in locating strings is impressive evidence for our belief that Rajan was encoding by location in a paired-associate fashion. Further support comes from the fact that it is not unusual for him to recall a sequence backward (specifying location of course). For example, Rajan recalled a four-digit string in which the last number was given first. He gave the location of the last number (Location 6), spoke the number then proceeded to give the locations and numbers of the preceding three digits in reverse order. It stretches credulity to suggest that he encodes a string by chunking according to prior knowledge and then recalls it backward.

   The data from these two extended recalls also provide some supporting evidence for the estimation of Rajan's basic memory span. When requested for the first extended recall, Rajan immediately gave the seven-digit sequence he had just recited. We attribute that recall to the recency of prior recall. With that exception, and another three-digit string that appeared in three of the presented spans (the shortest of which was 13 digits), he recalled no sequences from spans less than 15 digits in length. This suggests that he is not encoding spans of 14 digits or less in long-term memory.

   Finally, Rajan was once asked if he was ever bothered by sequences from previous days. Rajan replied that information from previous days was not a problem as he remembered only "bits and pieces" of those sequences. As an example, he recited 15 digits and said they were the last 15 digits from the 30-digit sequence that concluded the previous day's session. Upon checking, the experimenter found that Rajan had correctly given the final 15 digits from the last 30-digit sequence 2 days previous. Successful retrieval of the sequence after 48 hours again demonstrates deep encoding of portions of the memory span. Further, the length of the retrieved string is consistent with Rajan's claim that he encodes a memory span into sequences of 14–17 digits. Incidentally, we chided Rajan about his poor memory because he recalled the 15-digit string but not the date on which he heard it. He took our teasing with good humor.

PARALLEL PROCESSING

Because Rajan has great facility with numbers, we thought that he might not show the deficits normally shown when subjects do two tasks simultaneously. We drew on the theoretical description of working memory put forth by Baddeley and Hitch (1974) because they supplied substantial empirical evidence for their speculations together with proposing specific parallel processing procedures.

Baddeley and Hitch postulated that working memory consists of a central executive and a number of subsidiary slave systems. The two slave systems that they have described are visual (the visuospatial sketch pad) and verbal (the articulatory loop). Baddeley succinctly described the articulatory loop in his 1990 book. He pointed out that the articulatory loop involves a phonological store that holds information for about 2 seconds. That store operates together with an articulatory control process, which refreshes items in the store through subvocal rehearsal. It is also capable of recoding printed material to register it in the phonological store.

We selected two tasks to investigate Rajan's parallel processing ability. These tasks were memory load and articulatory suppression, which presumably produce performance deficits by overloading two different processes. The memory load task is hypothesized to overload the central executive, whereas the concurrent articulation task is hypothesized to overload the articulatory loop.

Memory Load

The first parallel processing task was selected to place a heavy load on the central executive component of working memory. The basic hypothesis is that working memory has a limited capacity and, thus, should show load effects in parallel processing procedures. We used the reasoning task developed by Baddeley (1968) and later used by Baddeley and Hitch (1974) as a memory load. Subjects were required to respond quickly (either *true* or *false*) to sentences of the form "A follows B–AB" while holding a digit span representing either 0, 20, 40, 60, or 80% of their normal digit span. Baddeley and Hitch (1974) showed that the time to solve the reasoning task increases as the digit span to be held approaches the normal digit span.

For the experiment, 32 sentences of the form "A precedes B–AB" were constructed by varying letter location in the sentence (A follows B vs. B follows A), letter location in the letter string (AB vs. BA), passive versus active sentences (is followed by vs. follows), precedes versus follows, and positive versus negative (follows vs. does not follow).

In each of four sessions, each subject received all 32 sentences under one of the load conditions (20, 40, 60, or 80% of span) and under the control (no load) condition. Thus, each subject received 64 sentences in each session with load and no-load conditions intermixed. The load conditions were presented in successive sessions. Ordinarily, the order of load conditions would be counterbalanced over subjects. In this case, it was important for the control subjects to operate under the same conditions as Rajan so they went through the same sequence as Rajan. We elected to present the loads in the sequence 20, 40, 60 and 80% of span. Because practice effects and amount of load were completely confounded, our focus in analysis will be on the difference between load and no-load conditions within a session.

Prior to the start of each trial, the subject was informed that the trial was either a load or a no-load trial. In the load conditions, the digit span was presented at a rate of 1 digit per second with the digits appearing in the center of the monitor screen. One second after the last digit, an asterisk appeared in the center of the screen. One second after that, the question to which the subject was to respond appeared.

The experimenter recorded the answer by hitting the appropriate key (*Y* or *N*) when the subject responded. The computer was programmed to record the solution time and whether the response was correct or incorrect.

Solution Times. Because of practice effects and day-to-day variation in an individual's performance, we chose to use the difference between mean solution times for the 32 sentences under control (no-load) and experimental (load) conditions as the major dependent measure. Only the solution times where the subject provided a correct solution and an errorless span were included in the means. Rajan's difference scores and the mean difference scores of the control subjects are shown in Table 2.2. As can be seen, the difference between load and no-load conditions increased systematically for control subjects as memory load increased. Although Rajan's data were more erratic, the difference between load and no-load conditions increased dramatically for the heaviest load condition.

Although the mean correct solution times under memory load were subject to practice effects, they are also of interest. Those means are also presented in Table 2.2. As can be seen, the mean correct solution time increased for the heaviest load, and that increase was particularly marked for Rajan.

Under no-load conditions, the mean errors in the reasoning task (with 32 attempts) were 1.0 and .7 for Rajan and the control subjects, respectively. The mean errors in the reasoning task under load conditions are also presented in Table 2.2. Rajan showed no systematic change in errors under load conditions, whereas the control subjects' errors increased systematically with increasing memory load. As might be expected, both Rajan and the control subjects made more errors in the load condition than in the no-load condition.

Keep in mind that heaviest load condition averaged 7 digits for the control subjects, whereas it was 28 digits for Rajan. Put differently, Rajan's lightest load (7) was the same length as the control subject's heaviest load.

Rajan's performance in the memory load experiment was as predicted by Baddeley's theory (e.g., Baddeley & Hitch, 1974). In this experiment, Rajan's per-

TABLE 2.2
Mean Difference in Solution Times for Memory Load and No-Load Conditions
Together with Mean Solution Times and Mean Errors under Load Conditions

	Memory Load (% of span)			
	20	40	60	80
Difference scores				
Rajan	.51	−.41	.74	4.03
Control Ss	.12	.22	.46	.62
Mean Solution Times				
Rajan	4.03	4.66	4.96	9.42
Control Ss	3.36	3.66	3.65	4.19
Mean Errors				
Rajan	5.0	4.0	2.0	5.0
Control Ss	.8	1.8	4.0	8.8

formance appeared to roughly parallel the performance of the control subjects. Thus, rather than being immune to the effects of a parallel processing task, his performance appeared to be comparable to the performance of ordinary subjects.

Articulatory Suppression

The second parallel processing task was selected to place a heavy load on the articulatory loop system. That system was postulated by Baddeley and Hitch (1974) as a part of working memory to account for certain articulatory effects. As one example, they found a deficit in working memory when the subject was required to respond "the, the, the, . . ." at a very rapid rate while performing the digit span task.

The control subjects were quite experienced at the memory span task at the time they did the articulatory suppression task. To be specific, they had completed at least 16 hours doing memory span.

During the articulatory suppression sessions, all subjects were instructed to repeat out loud the word "the" as rapidly as possible during the visual presentation of the digit span. We started each subject with a digit span equivalent to the mean performance on the last 10 trials of practice on visual digit span. Each successful recall incremented the span for the next trial by one digit, whereas each unsuccessful recall decremented the span on the next trial by one digit.

The control subjects began with 50 baseline trials (i.e., memory span trials without suppression). Then they were given 50 trials with articulatory suppression followed by at least 50 regular memory span trials. The sequence was then repeated with 50 more trials with the articulatory suppression instructions and 50 more regular memory span trials. Individual sessions lasted from ½ hour to 1½ hours, depending on availability for testing. The control subjects typically could complete 50 trials in ½ hour. With his greater memory span and breaks to minimize interference from prior trials, it took Rajan several sessions to complete 50 trials. Hence, following baseline trials, Rajan was given 70 trials with the articulatory suppression instructions followed by 30 trials of regular memory span. He participated in only one articulatory suppression series.

Suppression Data.   Baseline performance was calculated from the last 30 trials for Rajan and the final 50 regular trials for the control subjects. The articulatory suppression trials were grouped in blocks of 10 trials, and the average for each block was calculated.

The results of this experiment are presented separately for each subject in Figures 2.4 to 2.8. With the exception of DA during the first set of articulatory suppression trials, all subjects showed a drop in memory span during both articulatory suppression sessions. There was a tendency for subjects to recover, at least partially, from suppression. The control subjects exhibited maximum drops of 28% and 20% (measured from the baseline to the lowest level of performance) during the first and second articulatory suppression sessions, respectively. Rajan showed a maximum drop of 32%. Note that Rajan took longer to reach his lowest level of performance because he had longer to drop and the procedure only reduced the span by one digit on every unsuccessful trial.

Once again, Rajan performed as predicted by Baddeley's theory (e.g., Bad-

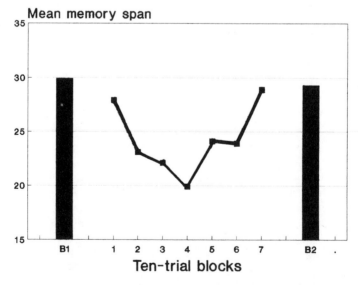

FIG. 2.4.   Mean memory span for Rajan under articulatory suppression. The data are presented separately for each 10-trial block. The baseline measure preceding articulatory suppression (B1) is the mean of 50 trials, whereas the baseline following articulatory suppression is the mean of 30 trials.

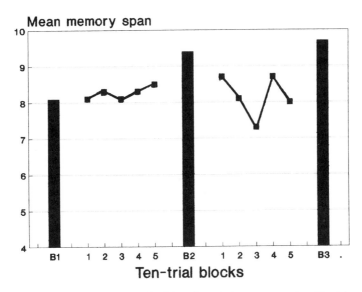

FIG. 2.5. Mean memory span for DA under articulatory suppression. The data are presented separately for each 10-trial block. Each baseline measure (B1, B2, and B3) is the mean of 50 trials.

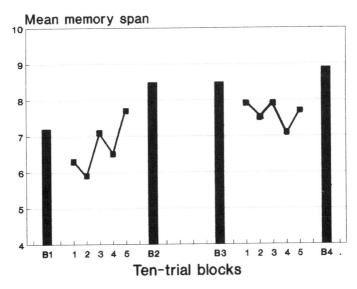

FIG. 2.6. Mean memory span for GN under articulatory suppression. The data are presented separately for each 10-trial block. Each baseline measure (B1, B2, B3 and B4) is the mean of 50 trials.

35

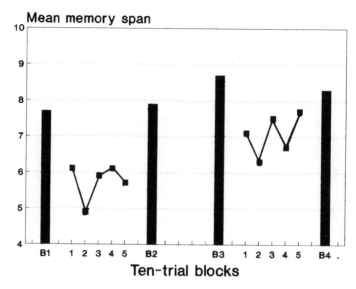

FIG. 2.7. Mean memory span for TH under articulatory suppression. The data are presented separately for each 10-trial block. Each baseline measure (B1, B2, B3 and B4) is the mean of 50 trials.

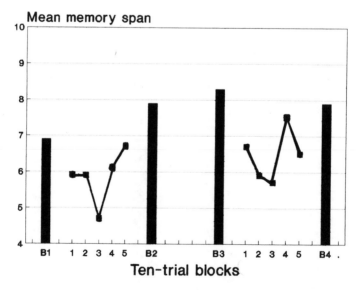

FIG. 2.8. Mean memory span for MD under articulatory suppression. The data are presented separately for each 10-trial block. Each baseline measure (B1, B2, B3 and B4) is the mean of 50 trials.

deley & Hitch, 1974). As in the memory load experiment, Rajan's performance essentially magnified the performance of subjects with ordinary memories.

RECOVERY FROM ARTICULATORY SUPPRESSION

The articulatory suppression data provided the one instance in which the performance of the control subjects was every bit as interesting as Rajan's performance. As noted previously, all subjects (including Rajan) appeared to recover from articulatory suppression. As we understand the Baddeley and Hitch theory, such recovery should not occur unless subjects were learning to increase their span during the articulatory suppression trials. In that case, one would expect an increased baseline span (i.e., on trials without articulatory suppression) following the articulatory suppression trials.

The evidence on increases in span (from the initial to the terminal baseline measure) and recovery from suppression was mixed. In the second run of trials, for example, DA and GN appeared to increase their memory span but TH and MD did not. Further, the first set of articulatory suppression trials seemed to strongly suggest recovery from suppression, whereas the data from the second series of articulatory suppression trials was not nearly as clear.

To get a clearer view of what appeared to be recovery from suppression, we decided to run our control subjects through a very long series of trials on the articulatory suppression procedure. During this period, Rajan was performing tests (e.g., a memory search of pi) in which the control subjects could not participate. To get a very stable indicator of memory span, we used the mean of 50-trial blocks as the measure of span. We began the experiment by deriving the baseline span using a 50-trial block. We then instituted the articulatory suppression trials. We kept a continuous record of performance (by 50-trial block) with the stipulation that we would stop the articulatory suppression trials when performance appeared to reach asymptote. At that point, we measured baseline span once again using a 50-trial block without articulatory suppression.

We were able to follow that strategy with three of our subjects. However, GN showed no sign of reaching asymptote, and we were not sure he would in a reasonable length of time. He had a baseline span of 13 digits when he began and had increased his baseline span to 17 digits when we stopped his trials. Probably because he was working with a relatively long span, he took much longer than other subjects for each session.

MD completed 800 trials under articulatory suppression. TH and DA each completed 700 trials under articulatory suppression. For the reasons noted before, GN only completed 200 trials with articulatory suppression.

The data for the articulatory suppression trials, together with the baseline trials preceding and following articulatory suppression are presented in Figs. 2.9, 2.10, 2.11, and 2.12 for DA, GN, TH, and MD, respectively.

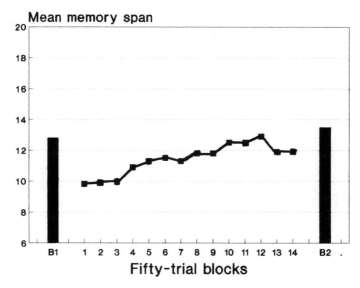

FIG. 2.9. Mean memory span for DA under articulatory suppression. The data are presented separately for each 50-trial block. Each baseline measure (B1 and B2) is the mean of 50 trials.

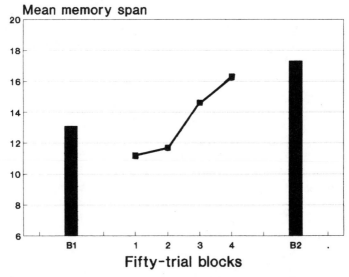

FIG. 2.10. Mean memory span for GN under articulatory suppression. The data are presented separately for each 50-trial block. Each baseline measure (B1 and B2) is the mean of 50 trials.

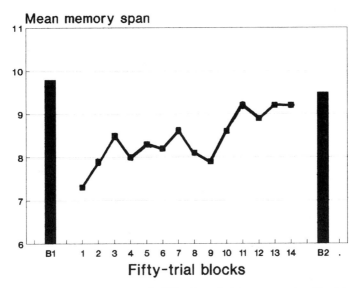

FIG. 2.11. Mean memory span for TH under articulatory suppression. The data are presented separately for each 50-trial block. Each baseline measure (B1 and B2) is the mean of 50 trials.

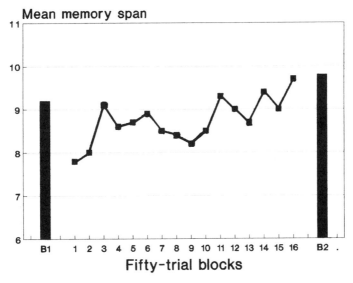

FIG. 2.12. Mean memory span for MD under articulatory suppression. The data are presented separately for each 50-trial block. Each baseline measure (B1 and B2) is the mean of 50 trials.

Recovery from articulatory suppression was evident for all subjects with the possible exception of GN. In his case, the reduction in memory span shown on the first block (from the initial baseline measure) is 13%. By contrast, the reduction in memory span shown on the last block (relative to the final baseline measure) is 8%. Even GN gives some evidence of a modest recovery from articulatory suppression.

Thus, these data show both articulatory suppression in the initial trials and recovery from articulatory suppression in later trials for all subjects. Clearly, articulatory suppression occurred. As predicted by Baddeley and Hitch (1974), the apparently irrelevant task of saying "the, the, the, . . ." at a rapid rate reduced performance on a memory span task. However, all subjects exhibited recovery during testing, and that would not be predicted by the Baddeley and Hitch theory.

The interesting question is how to interpret our subjects' recovery from suppression. One possibility is that their recovery might reflect a change from effortful to automatic processing. We might speculate that, while saying "the, the, the, ..." takes some work initially, the observed recovery indicates that this effortful task became automatic with practice. Another possibility is that the memory span task itself became more automatic and thus required less reliance on the articulatory loop slave system. In either case, we would speculate that a change to automatic processing would reduce the load on the articulatory control process with the presumed effect of reducing articulatory suppression.

However, it should be noted that the same cycle of suppression and recovery seemed to occur each time we tested our subjects. That cycle has two implications. First, because the memory span task occurs throughout baseline and articulatory suppression trials, the cycle eliminates changes in processing during the memory span task as a plausible explanatory mechanism. Second, the research on changes from effortful to automatic processing suggests that the change should be more permanent than indicated by the cycle in our data. Thus, we are not convinced that a switch from effortful to automatic processing is a useful way to explain why our subjects exhibited articulatory suppression each time we reimposed the task.

A further problem for Baddeley's theory is based on a few tests carried out later with one of our subjects who greatly increased his span (GN). After considerable practice, GN appeared to show no articulatory suppression when he was switched from straight memory span to memory span with articulation. Thus, it appears possible that some subjects may show no articulatory suppression effects after they have had considerable practice on the memory span task. We emphasize that automatic processing of the articulation task should reduce the load on the articulatory control process but have no effect on the corruption of the phonological store. Thus, the Baddeley and Hitch theory must predict some residual suppression effect.

We suggest a possibility that modifies, but does not discard, the elegant formulation by Baddeley and Hitch. We think that our subjects were able to bypass the articulatory loop mechanism and reserve it for the memory span task. To do so, they would need to use a portion of the central executive to run what became, for them, a background articulatory task. We suggest that it remained an effortful task. One of our subjects captured our speculation when he said that he was able to get past the interfering properties of the task by "listening to myself say 'the, the, the' in the back of my mind," thus distancing himself from the distraction. In addition, our later tests with GN raised the strong possibility that access to the phonological store is *not* obligatory. Put differently, it may be difficult, but not impossible, to restrict access to the phonological store.

A few comments about our subjects are worth noting. It should be obvious that we were dealing with quite sophisticated subjects with regard to the memory span task. When they completed the experiment just reported, our subjects had completed nearly 50 hours on the memory span task along with approximately double that time on other digit manipulation tasks; they were extremely sophisticated subjects. We suspect that it may be necessary to have well-practiced subjects such as ours to observe recovery from articulatory suppression. Indeed, we ran a few naive subjects for about 30 hours and found no evidence of recovery from articulatory suppression. We think these data suggest that the Baddeley and Hitch theory applies to naive subjects and also to subjects with a fair amount of practice, but it has to be modified to capture the performance of experts.

Non-Numeric Performance

In the last chapter, we showed that Rajan's performance on tasks involving the memorization of strings of digits is outstanding. The question is whether that skill transfers to other memory tasks. Research on skilled performance (e.g., Chase & Ericsson, 1981, 1982) suggests that such performance is restricted to a well-defined set of materials. Consistent with that research, we found that Rajan's memory span for digits increased to about 60 digits while his memory span for letters remained at approximately 13 letters.

The investigations described in this chapter have two thrusts. First, we wished to establish Rajan's level of performance on a variety of memory tasks. Second, we wished to determine whether his success at using a rather conceptually barren strategy on the digit string task would lead him to adopt similar strategies on tasks where such strategies would be inappropriate.

WORD LISTS

We speculated that Rajan's skill at remembering digit strings might affect the strategies he uses to recall lists of words. It is well established that normal subjects tend to organize the words for recall. When the words have an obvious categorical organization, subjects tend to organize by category (Bousfield, 1953) and their organization increases over trials and lists (Thompson & Roenker, 1971). Even when the material contains no obvious categories, subjects develop what Tulving (1962) dubbed *subjective organization*. We thought Rajan might modify or ignore the usual strategies employed by subjects.

Method

Three lists of low-frequency uncategorized words, three lists of high-frequency uncategorized words, and three lists of categorized words were constructed for use in this experiment. The uncategorized lists each contained 50 eight-letter two-syllable nouns. The words in the low-frequency and high-frequency lists had frequencies of 1 or above 50, respectively, in the Kucera and Francis (1967) norms. The frequency count ranged from 50 to 847 across the three high-frequency lists.

The categorized lists contained 49 words with seven words in each of seven categories. The categorized words had normative frequencies (Battig & Montague, 1969) ranging from 8 to 118 and were approximately matched across categories and lists. The Kucera and Francis frequency count ranged from 1 to 200 across the three categorized lists.

We presented the lists in the same order to all subjects so that Rajan and the control subjects could be compared. The low-frequency lists were presented first followed by the high-frequency lists and then the categorized lists. The ordering was deliberate in that we expected both learning-to-learn effects and the change in list type would produce a continuing increase in recall performance.

All subjects were given three trials on each of the lists. The words were presented in a different random order on each of the three trials. All lists were presented at a 2-second rate by a computer with each word appearing in the center of the monitor screen. Following presentation, a three-digit number appeared and the subjects counted backward by threes for 30 seconds prior to recall. Counting was introduced to eliminate the recency effect in recall. All subjects were given 4 minutes for recall on each trial.

Results

For reasons we do not understand, Rajan's performance on the third trial for the second categorized list was markedly abnormal. Specifically, he recalled only four words on that trial. Because that performance deviated so much from his performance on the other 26 trials (considering all conditions), we excluded that trial from these analyses.

Recall Data. Rajan differed from the control subjects both in amount recalled and in the strategy he used to recall. Consider first the recall data shown in Table 3.1. Both Rajan and the control subjects tended to improve recall as they moved from the low-frequency to the high-frequency lists. The control subjects improved even more when they recalled the categorized lists. By contrast, Rajan's performance on the categorized lists was equivalent to his performance on the low-frequency lists. He was clearly superior to all subjects on the uncategorized lists, but the control subjects were marginally better on the categorized lists.

TABLE 3.1
Mean Recall by Trial for Rajan and Control Ss on High-Frequency,
Low-Frequency, and Categorized Lists

	Low-Frequency	High-Frequency	Categorized
Control Ss			
Trial 1	11.3	16.3	24.0
2	21.9	24.4	34.9
3	26.3	32.0	41.1
Rajan			
Trial 1	13.0	20.0	13.3
2	25.7	34.3	25.0
3	36.0	42.3	35.0[a]

[a]List Two is not included in this mean.
Reprinted from Thompson et al. (1991), with permission.

Rajan's recall performance reflected a consistent strategy. He seemed to attend to the first 12–15 items presented, recite those on the first recall trial, and then rehearse those items during the remainder of the 4-minute recall period. On the second trial, he attended to an *additional* 12–15 items and recited the 24–30 total items on the second recall trial. On the third trial, he added another 12–15 items. Thus, his recall was fairly stereotyped: He ignored the structure of categorized lists, and he appeared to be aided by high-frequency exemplars.

Organizational Measures. Two organizational measures were used to capture Rajan's strategy. *Subjective organization* refers to the tendency of subjects to recall a list of unrelated words in the same order even though the list is presented in a different order on each trial. *Clustering* refers to the tendency of subjects to recall a list of categorizable words by category although the words are presented in a random order. We used Pelligrino's (1971) measure of subjective organization (ARC') for the unorganized lists and the ARC measure developed in our laboratory (Roenker, Thompson, & Brown, 1971) to measure the clustering in recall of the categorized material. In both measures, a score of one (1) indicates perfect organization and a score of zero (0) indicates that organization is occurring at a chance level. As can be seen in Table 3.2, ARC' improved very little, if at all for control subjects as they went from low-frequency to high-frequency lists.

By contrast, Rajan's recall of unorganized material was very structured: His ARC' scores improved substantially as he went from low-frequency to high-frequency lists, and his ARC' scores on all noncategorized lists were much higher than any of the control subjects.

The data for the categorized lists clearly demonstrate that Rajan ignored the

TABLE 3.2
Mean Organization Measures (ARC and ARC′) by Trial for Rajan and
Control Ss on High-Frequency, Low-Frequency, and Categorized Lists

	Control Ss			Rajan		
Trial	1	2	3	1	2	3
Low-Freq. (ARC′)	–	.16	.17	–	.47	.32
High-Freq. (ARC′)	–	.22	.21	–	.74	.69
Categorized (ARC)	.73	.72	.76	.04	.13	.08[a]
Categorized (ARC′)	–	.18	.29	–	.64	.23[a]

[a]List Two is not included in these means.
Reprinted from Thompson et al. (1991), with permission.

structure of organized material. The control subjects' ARC′ scores for categorized material were around .75, whereas Rajan's ARC′ scores were around .10.

Because Rajan obviously ignored the categories in these lists, we also calculated the subjective organization measure (ARC′) for the categorized lists. Those
data are also presented in Table 3.2. As can be seen, the ARC′ scores for the
control subjects were comparable to the uncategorized lists on Trial 2 but appeared to be superior to the uncategorized lists on Trial 3. On Trial 2, Rajan
showed the same high degree of subjective organization (i.e., ARC′) that he
showed on the uncategorized lists. His ARC′ performance dropped markedly
on Trial 3. It is worth noting that his performance was relatively high on one
list (.53) and below chance (−.07) on the other list. The reason for his below
chance performance in that one instance is unclear.

Conclusions

Rajan's performance tracked the frequency characteristics of the three types of
lists rather than the organizational characteristics of the lists. Both Rajan and the
control subjects improved performance as they went from low-frequency to high-
frequency lists. The control subjects took advantage of the organization possible
with the categorized lists and improved their performance even more. In contrast, Rajan's performance reflected the lower word-frequency count of the categorized list as his performance dropped to the level he had produced on the
low-frequency lists.

The categorized list data are a good example of a situation in which Rajan's
skilled memory does not produce outstanding performance. He ignored the available structure of the categorized list and relied instead on an approach that capital-
ized on his strong rote memory. In this case, his rote memory ability was not
able to exceed the advantage provided for ordinary subjects by the categorized
structure of the word lists.

STORY MEMORY

Rajan's unusual approach to learning word lists led us to wonder how he would perform on ordinary text. The story often used for this purpose is Bartlett's *War of the Ghosts* story (Bartlett, 1932). It is used because its unusual structure makes it difficult to remember. We were unable to use that story because Rajan had been exposed to it in class and tested on it earlier. Instead, we used three Eskimo stories which maintained many of the unusual characteristics of Bartlett's classic story. The Eskimo stories were titled *Kayatuq the Red Fox, The Dog Wife,* and *Nakkayaq and his Sister.* All three stories were taken from Rice (1980).

Method

Each story was presented at a separate testing session. All subjects were allowed to read each story through twice at their own pace with total reading time recorded for each story. After reading each story twice, the subjects worked on other tasks for 45 minutes, and then they were asked to produce a written version of the story. They were instructed to be as accurate as possible in their reconstruction. The recalled version of each story for each subject was transferred to the computer so that multiple typed copies of each recall could be produced for scoring purposes.

Results

The Eskimo stories were scored for recall of idea units based on the propositional analysis advocated by Kintsch (1974). The complete set of idea units was developed for each story prior to scoring that story. Each recall for each subject was scored separately by two experimenters. The two scoring protocols were compared with any disagreements resolved by a third experimenter. The data are presented in Table 3.3. As can be seen, Rajan's recall performance was typically low or intermediate compared to the control subjects. His study times were also within the range produced by the control subjects. The one exception was the *Red Fox* story in which Rajan took a very long time to study the story but produced an intermediate recall score. Clearly, Rajan's forte is not memory for prose. He learns such material as well as ordinary subjects.

COMPLEX FIGURES TASK

Rajan states that he does not use imagery in memorizing numbers or words, and his performance seems consistent with that statement. We thought it important, therefore, to assess his performance on a task in which good imagery would be

TABLE 3.3
Mean Study Time and Recall of Idea Units Presented Separately for
Each Control Subject and for Rajan for Each Eskimo Story

	Idea Units Recalled		
	Dog Wife	Sister	Red Fox
(Possible)	(60)	(77)	(71)
Rajan	42	30	52
GN	31	41	34
TH	32	45	35
MD	48	65	59
DA	49	68	63
	Study Time (in seconds)		
	Dog Wife	Sister	Red Fox
Rajan	277	249	593
GN	175	202	248
TH	132	145	107
MD	258	227	241
DA	279	325	239

Reprinted from Thompson et al. (1991), with permission.

extremely helpful. For that purpose, we selected the Rey–Osterrieth Complex Figure Test (Osterrieth, 1944; Rey, 1942), which was developed to measure visual–spatial memory. This test was used because the figures appear to be so complex that simple verbal coding of the figures would be difficult.

Method

In this task, a complex figure was placed in front of the subject. He or she was instructed to copy the figure as accurately as possible. The subject was also informed that he or she would be asked to reproduce the figure at a later time. After the figure had been copied, the experimenter asked the subject to double check his or her drawing to make sure it was complete and accurate. The experimenter then removed the figure from sight and recorded the time taken to copy and check the figure. A maximum of 10 minutes was allowed for the subject to copy the figure. The subject performed a nonrelated memory task (digit memory span) for a period of 30 minutes.

Following the 30-minute interval, the subject was asked to reproduce as much of the figure from memory as he or she possibly could. When the subject indicated the drawing was finished, the subject was asked to make sure the figure was complete and accurate. Following this, it was removed from sight, and the time taken to reproduce the figure was recorded. Immediately following reproduction of the first figure, this procedure was repeated for a second complex figure.

Following a 48-hour interval from the time the figure had been copied, the subject was asked again to reproduce the first figure from memory. The procedure for reproduction of the figure after 48 hours was identical to the procedure for reproduction of the figure after 30 minutes. After reproducing the first figure from memory, the subject was asked to reproduce the second figure.

Results

A procedure for scoring the data was described by Taylor (1959). Briefly, each figure was divided into 18 units with each unit assigned two points if it was correctly reproduced; one point if it was misplaced, incomplete, or distorted; one-half point if it was recognizable but misplaced and incomplete or distorted; and no points were awarded for a unit absent or unrecognizable.

Rajan's accuracy scores and times to copy and reproduce from memory both figures are given in Table 3.4 together with the mean scores for the control subjects. Rajan's performance on the first figure was virtually identical to the mean performance for the control subjects. In both production time and accuracy in all conditions, Rajan's data was somewhere in the middle of control group performance.

TABLE 3.4
Mean Production Times in Minutes and Accuracy Scores for Rajan and the
Control Ss on the Complex Figure Task

		Recall	
	Copy	*30 min*	*48 hr*
Figure I			
Production Time			
Rajan	5.0	4.0	2.0
Control Ss	5.9	2.8	3.1
Accuracy Score			
Rajan	35.0	30.5	28.0
Control Ss	34.5	30.1	28.8
Figure II			
Production Time			
Rajan	8.0	4.0	3.0
Control Ss	5.8	2.8	3.3
Accuracy Score			
Rajan	36.0	33.0	32.0
Control Ss	35.0	31.1	28.0

Reprinted from Thompson et al. (1991), with permission.

The data for the second figure showed a slight improvement in Rajan's performance. If Rajan's performance on the second figure is compared with the means for the control subjects, his accuracy was slightly higher on both copy and reproduction. However, he took 60% more time copying the second figure than he did copying the first figure. Further, although Rajan scored slightly higher than the mean of the control subjects, his performance was nearly identical to that of the two best control subjects. As would be expected, all subjects typically showed a decline in their accuracy of reproduction with time. The data provide evidence that Rajan does not have an exceptional memory for figures that are visually complex.

Rajan's description of the strategy used to copy and reproduce the figures relied less on visual imagery than the strategies described by several of the control subjects. Rajan reported that each of the figures were composed of several quadrants. He scanned the figure for symmetrical properties, such as the number of lines in a quadrant. He also reported that certain structures within one quadrant would be in alignment with structures in another quadrant. In contrast to Rajan's analytical approach was the high-imagery strategy reported by TH. She reported that if you turn the first figure on its side the figure looked like a house with a TV antenna, a kite flying on the top (complete with a tail), and a tiny face inside. Another subject, DA, used a similar high-imagery approach. When he turned the first figure on its side, he saw a barn with doors in the front and a flag on the top. In the second figure, DA saw a spider (the asterisk) and its web in the upper left corner. One common strategy used by all of the subjects was to draw the large rectangle first, draw the large triangles second, split the rectangle into sections, and then add the details. The analytic strategy used by Rajan supports his claim that he does not use imagery when memorizing various types of material.

PSYCHOMETRIC PROFILE

Jeanne Frieman from Kansas Neurological Institute assisted us in getting a psychometric profile of Rajan. She used two tests for that purpose. As the initial test, she used the Leiter International Performance Scale in an attempt to take into account Rajan's bilingual status and Indian nationality. That test showed weaknesses in visual motor ability and visual concept formation with an overall IQ of 114. He showed his best performance when he could translate the task into a verbal task using primarily auditory cues.

The tasks that caused him difficulty were appreciating similar visual form (not identity), analogous facial expressions, very complex block designs, and appreciating relative dot density. In the latter task, he attempted to count the dots and failed to be able to maintain a starting point. Rajan had difficulty choosing an optimal approach to very difficult tasks and tended to attempt to translate every task into his preferred strategy even if that strategy did not work well for all tasks.

The 1986 revision of the Stanford–Binet Intelligence Scale was also administered. This scale divides skills into four groups: Quantitative Reasoning, Verbal Reasoning, Abstract Visual Reasoning, and Short-Term Memory. The memory section has two subtests that address auditory memory and two that assess visual memory skills. Rajan's performance demonstrated his weakness in the area of visual reasoning. Indeed, he showed the profile of an individual with a visual motor learning disability. His other scores fell in the average to above-average range. The short-term memory section showed a sharp distinction between visual and auditory memory performance. Rajan showed only average memory performance on the visual subtests but showed superior performance on the auditory subtests.

The findings of the Stanford–Binet evaluation indicated that Rajan has unusually good auditory memory. While performing, Rajan generally reported that he visualizes material he learns. However, these test results suggest his skill involves unusual auditory, rather than visual, memory.

CONCLUSIONS

Visual Imagery

Rajan's comments (during his psychometric evaluation) that he visualizes the material he learns were quite surprising to us. Rajan was most emphatic with us in stating that his exceptional performance with digits does not depend on visual imagery. The data presented in this chapter provide support for this claim; his recall of complex figures was unexceptional, and his psychometric profile showed weaknesses on visual tasks.

After our tests were administered, additional evidence was collected regarding Rajan's performance on visual tasks. In a specific test of spatial memory, Biederman, Cooper, Fox, and Mahadevan (1992) showed that Rajan's performance was lower than that of eight control subjects. Another series of tests on Rajan (Baddeley, Mahadevan, & Thompson, 1992) included visual memory span, a visual recognition test (the Doors test), and a visual recall test. Consistent with our results, Rajan scored lowest (or tied for low) on visual memory span and the visual recognition test. The visual recall test was not informative because Rajan and three of the six control subjects performed at ceiling on this test.

Taken together, the evidence strongly supports Rajan's contention that he does not use visual imagery in learning or reciting numeric material. Indeed, the evidence demonstrates that the conclusion put forth in the psychometric profile is correct—Rajan is, at best, average on visual tasks and probably has a deficit in visual imagery.

Encoding Strategy

These data also tend to support an observation that we find most remarkable. Rajan's encoding strategy seems to be barren; that is, he appeared to attach a minimum of meaning when encoding a string of digits. As we noted in chapter 2, he did not ignore meaningful strings when they appeared (e.g., according to Rajan, the string 111 is a "Nelson" because Rajan thought that Admiral Nelson had one eye, one arm, and one leg). However, his use of those meaningful strings appeared to be arbitrary and incidental rather than a central aspect of his encoding strategy.

Rajan was very successful at, and earned a great deal of attention from, encoding long strings of numbers. By any measure, his strategy for encoding digits succeeded. Therefore, we might reasonably expect him to carry that strategy over to other tasks that involve encoding large amounts of material. Given that expectation, what was particularly striking about Rajan's performance on the tasks reported in this chapter was his consistent failure to attempt to attach meaning to the tasks.

Rajan was alone among the subjects in his mechanical description of the Rey–Osterreith figures. One might attribute his approach on the Rey–Osterreith figures to his poor imagery, but that explanation fails when attempting to describe his poor performance on the categorized word lists. A more consistent explanation is that Rajan depended on a strategy dominated by rote learning. That strategy served him well when rote learning was appropriate (e.g., with lists of unrelated words). His strategy failed when some meaning could be attached to the verbal material (e.g., categorized word lists, stories) or to the visual material (e.g. the Rey–Osterreith figures). When meaning could be attached to the material to be remembered, Rajan's performance was inferior, or at best equal, to that of the control subjects.

The data reported here are consistent with the data from tests of Rajan's memory span. In those studies, Rajan appeared to focus on the location of a sequence in the span and essentially learned the sequence by rote. Rote learning of a series of digits is a daunting task, and we are surprised to find no evidence for any consistent effort to attach meaning to strings of numbers.

CHAPTER 4

Number Matrices

Rajan often chooses to learn and recite a matrix of numbers during a public performance. His facility in this task is very impressive. When given an opportunity to ask questions, people focus on three characteristics related to his performance: Their questions make it clear that they believe some sort of "photographic memory" must be necessary to perform the feat. In addition, they usually ask whether he uses a mnemonic to remember the digits. Finally, they want to know how long he remembers the matrix.

We consider those three issues in this chapter. Our research shows conclusively that Rajan does not have a "photographic memory" and strongly suggests that he does not use a mnemonic to learn the digits. Further, we show that Rajan must rehearse matrices in order to retain them. In addition, we present an interesting finding: Rajan can learn matrices when the digits comprising the matrix are presented in a random order. His performance on the randomly presented matrices suggests the strategy Rajan uses in learning matrices.

MATRIX LEARNING AND RETENTION

Experiment 1: Matrix Learning

Rajan's description of the process he uses to memorize digits, as well as his performance on some standardized tests, suggest that he does not use a visual process. Binet reported a simple procedure to distinguish between visual and verbal encoding (Ericsson, 1988). He used it in testing the memorists Inaudi and Diamondi.

Binet had them learn matrices of digits and then called for recall of specific rows and columns in the matrices as well as diagonal and spiral recall. Binet reasoned that a visual image would make it equally easy to recall any spatially organized subset of information in the matrix such as rows, diagonals, or columns. Put differently, the subject should be able to read directly from the visual image.

Using the same logic to test for strong visual imagery, we had Rajan (and our controls) learn a large set of single-digit matrices and then tested them on their ability to recall the rows and columns of those matrices. In addition to testing for strong visual imagery, we wished to measure Rajan's current ability level in learning number matrices and determine whether he would increase his speed of learning matrices as predicted by Chase and Ericsson (1981, 1982).

For this experiment, we constructed five matrices each of sizes 5 × 5, 7 × 7, 9 × 9, 10 × 10, 14 × 14, and 20 × 20; thus, the total digits in these matrices ranged from 25 to 400. All matrices were constructed using a random number generator on the microcomputer. In addition, eight matrices for each of two additional matrix sizes (6 × 6 and 12 × 12) were constructed to study recall of matrix rows and columns.

All subjects were presented all matrices up to size 10 × 10. Based on pilot studies, we set 1 hour as an upper limit for matrix learning. We set the limit because we wished to keep the same set of control subjects we had already used in many tasks. One of our control subjects found matrix learning very aversive and probably would have left the project had we increased the difficulty of the task. Because some control subjects took longer than 1 hour to learn the larger matrices, only Rajan was given the 12 × 12, 14 × 14, and 20 × 20 matrices. The matrices were presented in a random order with the restriction that all the different matrix sizes were exhausted before beginning another set of presentations. Sessions were restricted to 1 hour with subjects completing as many matrices as possible within that time.

Subjects were given the matrix printed and centered on an ordinary sheet of computer paper. They studied the matrix until they felt they could repeat it without error. At that point, they returned the matrix to the experimenter and attempted recall. The experimenter recorded the study and recall time as well as any errors in recall.

Following recall of each 6 × 6 matrix, all subjects were asked to recall individual rows and columns from the matrix. The subjects were given a randomly selected set of three rows and three columns to recall. These were given one at a time in a random order and the subject did not know which row (or column) would be requested. The row and column positions were randomly sampled without replacement so that each row and column had been tested when a block of two 6 × 6 matrices was completed. Recall time and errors, if any, were recorded for each recall attempt. Rajan followed the same program of testing for the 12 × 12 matrices except that only the odd rows and columns were tested.

Time to Learn Matrices.   Mean time per digit (in seconds) to learn all matrices is shown in Fig. 4.1. As would be expected, the time per digit increased with the number of digits to be learned. Within the range used (matrices of 25 to 100 digits), the increase was essentially linear for the control subjects. The range used for Rajan was much larger (25–400 digits), but the time per digit for Rajan also increased linearly for matrices of size 9 × 9 through 20 × 20. We excluded the smaller matrices from consideration because Rajan had successfully completed memory span tests exceeding the number of digits in those matrices. Thus, we thought it possible that his strategy for those matrices might differ from the strategy he used to learn the larger matrices.

As matrix size increased, time per digit appeared to increase for control subjects at a rate of about 2.3 seconds for every 25 digits added. By contrast, Rajan's time per digit increased at a rate of .7 seconds for every additional 25 digits.

In summary, compared to the control subjects, Rajan learned digits three times more rapidly and was less affected by increasing the number of digits to be learned. As one example of the striking difference between Rajan and the control subjects, his per-digit rate while learning 400 digits was about the same as or less than the control subjects' per-digit rate while learning 25 digits.

As shown in Fig. 4.1, Rajan learned number matrices of about 50 digits at a rate of 1.7 seconds per digit. Rajan's rate of learning number matrices was not only faster than our control subjects, it also was faster than the rates recorded for other well-known memorists (see chapter 8).

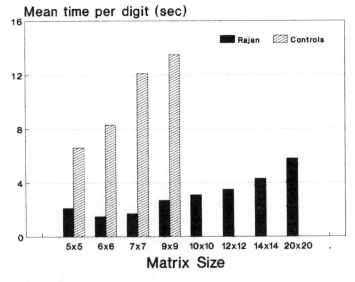

FIG. 4.1.   Mean time per digit to learn each matrix size presented separately for Rajan and the control subjects.

Error Data. Rajan made only four errors in reciting the 46 matrices. He gave a single incorrect digit on a 12 × 12 matrix and also on a 20 × 20 matrix. He omitted a digit on a different 12 × 12 matrix. Finally, he reversed a three-digit sequence on still another 12 × 12 matrix. He made no errors on the matrices that also were learned by the control subjects.

The control subjects attempted to recite 28, rather than 46, matrices. They exhibited a wide range of error performance. The best control subject made a single error on one of the 5 × 5 matrices. The worst control subject found the task very aversive and made extensive errors on all of the larger (9 × 9 and 10 × 10) matrices. That subject also made one or more errors on six of the 18 remaining matrices. The other two control subjects made errors on five and seven matrices, respectively.

Rate of Recitation. Rajan prefers to recite items at the speed at which he recited the first 10,000 digits of pi—that is, at approximately 5 digits per second. After a few trials, we requested that he slow down so that our verification of his recitation would be accurate. His slow rate of recitation is typically about 2.5 digits per second. The important point about his rapid rate of recitation is that it would seem to rule out any possibility that he is using some sort of conscious mnemonic to reproduce the strings of numbers.

Recall of Rows and Columns. The data for recall of the rows and columns of the 6 × 6 matrix are shown in Fig. 4.2. The comparable data for the 12 × 12 matrix are shown in Fig. 4.3.

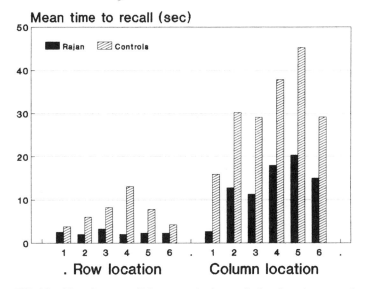

FIG. 4.2. Mean time to recall the rows and columns of a 6 × 6 matrix presented separately for Rajan and the control subjects.

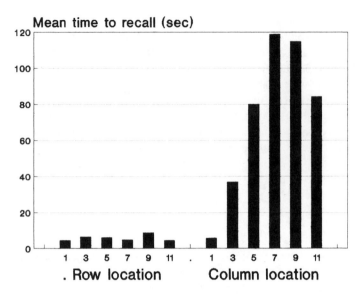

FIG. 4.3. Mean time to recall the odd-numbered rows and columns of a 12 × 12 matrix. These data are from Rajan.

There are several points to be made about Rajan's recall of the rows and columns of the matrices: These data strongly suggest that Rajan's recall did not depend on some visual image of the matrix. If it did, his time to recall rows and columns should have been roughly equivalent because he could have read the row or column from the visual image. While reading habit might produce faster row recitation, it could not account for the difference found in Figs. 4.2 and 4.3. As can be seen in the figures, Rajan's recall of columns was substantially slower than his recall of rows.

His recall of rows was fast and did not differ greatly with location in the 6 × 6 matrix. Because there are more digits to be produced in the larger matrix, it is not surprising that Rajan's recall time for a row was longer for the larger matrix. The control subjects also took systematically longer to recall the interior rows of the 6 × 6 matrix.

In contrast to row recall, Rajan's recall of columns was relatively slow and became markedly slower across columns. This effect is shown clearly in the data for both matrix sizes. The right-most column tested in both matrices was an exception in that recall for that column, while slow in comparison to the rows, was much faster than recall for the two immediately preceding columns of the matrix. Rajan stated that he found it easiest to produce the right-most tested column in the two matrices by recalling the entire row and then giving the last digit in the 6 × 6 matrix or, in the 12 × 12 matrix, "backing up" one digit to produce the penultimate digit.

In summary, the data support Rajan's statement that he learns a matrix by rows and recalls columns by taking the appropriate digit from each row. The exception is the first column, which he memorizes as an aid to keep track of rows during recall.

The control subjects' recall of columns showed the same pattern as Rajan: Recall time increased with column number except for the last column. Considering both rows and columns, the recall data suggest that the control subjects learned the matrices in much the same way as Rajan.

Effect of Practice.   Chase and Ericsson (1981, 1982) proposed that one of the characteristics of skilled memory is that performance speeds up with practice. The matrix data provide a test of that hypothesis because subjects were presented the matrices in successive sets with each set including all matrix sizes. In this analysis, we measured the mean time per matrix to learn each matrix set. The mean of those means are presented separately for each subject in Table 4.1. As can be seen, Rajan shows a systematic decrease over sets in the mean time per matrix to learn a matrix set. By contrast, the control subjects showed no such systematic change. For three of the four control subjects, the fourth set of matrices took the longest time to learn.

Encoding Procedure.   Rajan has stated that he learns a matrix by rows and also learns the first column as a method to order the rows. The data presented here support his verbal report. Rows are recalled rapidly upon request with row location producing little variation in time to recall. By contrast, all columns but the first are recalled relatively slowly and time to recall varies substantially with column position. Most importantly, the first column is recalled with the same speed as most rows and is recalled faster than some rows.

Rajan's description suggests that he learns each row in a matrix as a chunk. We assumed that he might use smaller strings of numbers (e.g., 5–9 digits) as

TABLE 4.1

Mean Time Per Matrix (in Seconds) to Learn the Matrices in a Set Presented Separately for Each S and Each Set. The Matrix Sizes in Each Set Were 5 × 5, 6 × 6, 7 × 7, 9 × 9, and 10 × 10 for the Controls. The Matrix Sets for Rajan Included 12 × 12, 14 × 14, and 20 × 20 Matrices in Addition to the Matrix Sizes Already Noted.

| | Ordinal Position of Set | | | | |
	1	*2*	*3*	*4*	*5*
Rajan	673	586	562	487	455
DA	689	612	531	645	584
TH	641	619	684	827	563
GN	386	439	429	463	393
MD	765	760	871	1072	818

Reprinted from Thompson et al. (1991), with permission.

a chunk and string those together to complete a row. Thus, we attempted in a later study to identify chunks in matrix recall by recording Rajan's recall of matrices and listening for pauses in recitation. The recorded matrices ranged in size from 5 × 5 to 20 × 20. We found no systematic pauses other than at the end of a row. We concluded that Rajan treats the row as a chunk — at least in matrices of size 20 × 20 or less.

The important theoretical point is that Rajan's verbal report, the recall times for rows and columns, and an attempt to use pauses in recall to identify chunks all suggest that he uses the entire row as a chunk. Unlike the subjects studied by Chase and Ericsson (e.g., 1981,1982), Rajan does not appear to relate number sequences to earlier information. He appears to treat rows in a matrix much like he treats a memory span sequence. That is, he keeps track of the location (serial position) of each digit and learns the sequence as a cohesive series. The evidence is quite clear that he does not encode a matrix visually.

Experiment 2: Six-Month Retention

Rajan claimed that, once he had successfully retrieved a set of numbers, his memory for the set lasted for about 6 months and then began to fade. We were interested in whether his perception of his memory was accurate. His claim seemed entirely plausible because other memorists such as Shereshevskii (Luria, 1968) and VP (Hunt & Love, 1972) appeared to remember the material used in experimental sessions over long periods of time. For example, Luria reported giving Shereshevskii unexpected recall tests on word lists 15 or 16 years after he originally recalled the list. Luria stated that Shereshevskii was invariably successful in retrieving the entire list (p. 12).

We had some evidence that Rajan is capable of maintaining sets of matrices for a long period. He had returned to Minnesota after an interval of 8½ years for some retesting. Although we do not have access to the initial or retest data, we were told that Rajan recalled without error the first four matrices on which he had been tested. We were told that those matrices ranged in size from 50 digits to 256 digits (a 16 × 16 matrix). We also were told that he made several errors on other matrices and had forgotten some of them completely.

Given what we knew about Rajan, it seemed unlikely to us that he would have physically recorded the Minnesota matrices but likely that he would have rehearsed at least some of them. We speculated that his memory for the first four Minnesota matrices might have resulted from occasional rehearsal. Unfortunately, because we had talked with Rajan about the duration of his memory, it seemed likely that he was anticipating a test of his ability. Rajan likes to perform well on such tests, so we were concerned that he might rehearse the matrices he had been given in anticipation of subsequent testing.

We decided to counter that possibility with some mild deception. In this experiment, we gave Rajan an initial retention test on some matrices (from Experiment 1) together with the suggestion that we had completed the tests of his ability to retain number matrices. In a series of subsequent experiments, we gave Rajan several unannounced memory tests. We thought the later tests would be a better measure of his memory for matrices. As will be seen, the pattern of data tends to support our speculation that he anticipated the retention tests reported in this experiment.

We were not concerned about Rajan physically recording the matrices because rehearsal seemed adequate to keep whatever numeric information Rajan wanted at hand. In the 4 years we knew him, we never saw any evidence to indicate that Rajan recorded numeric information.

Our first retention test occurred 6 months after Rajan learned the set of matrices described in Experiment 1. For convenience, we identify the set of matrices used in each experiment with the corresponding number (e.g., the matrices used in Experiment 1 are designated as Matrix Set One).

Twenty-four matrices, designated Matrix Set Two, were used for the first retention test. The set consisted of four matrices each of sizes 5 × 5, 7 × 7, 9 × 9, 10 × 10, 14 × 14, and 20 × 20. Two matrices of each size were the second and fifth matrices of that size presented in Experiment 1. The other two matrices of each size were new matrices. The pattern (but not the order) of matrix presentation is shown in Table 4.2. As in the first experiment, Rajan learned all the matrices while the control subjects only learned the matrices up to size 10 × 10.

The procedure in the retention experiments was the same as in Experiment 1 with two exceptions: (a) We did not test for rows and columns during the retention experiments, and (b) a recognition (and contingent recall) test was performed upon the initial presentation of each matrix.

The subject was shown the first line of each matrix and given a maximum of 10 seconds to indicate whether the matrix had been previously presented. If the answer was "no," the subject was shown the entire matrix and given an additional 10 seconds to indicate whether the matrix had been previously presented.

If the response was "yes" to either query, the subject immediately was asked

TABLE 4.2
Chart Illustrating the Pattern, but Not the Order, of Matrix Presentation in Each Experiment. This Pattern Occurred for Each of the Six Matrix Sizes. Underlined Matrices Represent the Old Matrices (i.e., Those Being Tested for Retention) in Each Set.

Experiment	Matrix Number Presented										
1	1	2	3	4	5						
2		$\underline{2}$			$\underline{5}$	6	7				
3			$\underline{3}$	$\underline{4}$		$\underline{6}$	$\underline{7}$	8	9		
4	$\underline{1}$							$\underline{8}$	$\underline{9}$	10	11

to recall as much of the matrix as possible. If recall was not successful, the subject was given the sheet of paper containing the matrix and the procedure continued as in the initial experiment.

Recognition Data. On this 6-month retention test, Rajan recognized all 12 of the matrices taken from the initial set. He recognized 10 of the 12 matrices based on presentation of the first line of the matrix. He could identify eight of them by number, and he said another was either matrix number 37 or 38 (it was number 38). He had only one false alarm.

In contrast, only two of the control subjects recognized any of the eight matrices they had studied, and those subjects had false alarm rates roughly equivalent to their hit rates. GN correctly identified one of the matrices but gave false alarms to three others. MD identified five of the matrices but also gave false alarms to three matrices. The false alarm rate demonstrates that these control subjects could not accurately discriminate between old and new matrices.

Recall Data. Whereas none of the control subjects could recall any of the matrices from Matrix Set One, Rajan had complete recall for eight of the matrices (both of the 5 × 5, 7 × 7, and 10 × 10 matrices, and one each of the 9 × 9 and 14 × 14 matrices). The recognition and recall data are summarized in Table 4.3.

Relearning Data. Rajan also showed savings scores of 60% for the other 9 × 9 matrix and 65% for the other 14 × 14 matrix. Interestingly, he could not relearn either of the 20 × 20 matrices within the allotted hour even though he recognized them and initially learned them within 42 minutes. Apparently, he was so shaken by his inability to recall them that he could not concentrate well enough to relearn them.

We should note, however, that the failure to show savings was not restricted to Rajan. When we calculated the savings scores for each matrix for the control subjects, each subject showed both negative and positive savings scores. The savings scores ranged from −67% to 53%. We were frankly surprised and even a bit dismayed when the savings score turned out to be an insensitive and extremely variable measure of retention.

Rajan's retention of the initial matrix set was quite impressive. The remaining question was whether that performance could be attributed to rehearsal.

Experiment 3: Twelve-Month Retention

Six months after the retention test just described, we gave all the subjects another retention test. We hoped to catch Rajan by surprise.

In this memory test, one-third of the matrices were from Matrix Set One, one-third of the matrices were from Matrix Set Two, and one-third were new. The

TABLE 4.3
Recall and Recognition Performance for Each Matrix Set Presented Separately for
Rajan and Each of the Control Subjects

Matrix Set One					
	Rajan	*GN*	*DA*	*TH*	*MD*
(N)	(12)	(8)	(8)	(8)	(8)
6 month					
Recognition	12	1	0	0	0
False Alarms	1	3	0	0	0
Complete Recall	8	0	NA	NA	NA
12 month					
Recognition	11	2	0	0	
False Alarms	0	0	0	0	
Complete Recall	0	0	NA	NA	
14 month (N)	(6)				
Recognition	6				
False Alarms	0				
Complete Recall	1				

Matrix Set Two				
	Rajan	*GN*	*DA*	*TH*
(N)	(12)	(8)	(8)	(8)
6 month				
Recognition	7	0	0	0
False Alarms	4	0	0	0
Complete Recall	1	NA	NA	NA

Matrix Set Three	
	Rajan
(N)	(12)
14 month	
Recognition	7
False Alarms	5
Complete Recall	0

pattern of matrices is also shown in Table 4.2. Rajan was given 36 matrices, and the control subjects were given 24 matrices. There were six matrices each of sizes 5×5, 7×7, 9×9, 10×10, 14×14, and 20×20. The 12 matrices from Matrix Set One were the third and fourth presented for each size in Experiment 1. These matrices were tested for 12-month retention. The 12 matrices that were new in Matrix Set Two were tested for 6-month retention. As before, Rajan learned all the matrices and the control subjects learned the matrices up to and including the 10×10 matrix. The procedure was identical to that used in Experiment 2. One of the control subjects withdrew from the experiment at this point because she moved from the area.

Recognition and Recall Data. The recognition and recall data for this experiment are also presented in Table 4.3. After 12 months, Rajan recognized 11 of the 12 matrices from Matrix Set One; however, he could no longer recall the identifying numbers of the matrices nor could he recall any of the matrices. Only one of the control subjects could either recognize or recall any matrices after 12 months. That subject recognized 2 of the 8 matrices with no false alarms.

We were much more interested in the data which we thought might represent an unexpected recall task. Thus we focus on the data for the 12 matrices presented for the first time 6 months earlier. As can be seen, Rajan's recognition performance was still very good; he identified 7 of the 12 matrices with four false alarms. However, in contrast to his earlier retention test, he could not identify any of the matrices by number.

His recall performance was considerably poorer than on the original retention test as he recalled only one of the 12 matrices. His recall of that matrix must be viewed with doubt for two reasons: First, he did not recognize the matrix as a matrix previously presented, and second, it is clearly possible for him to learn a matrix of that size (5 × 5) in the two 10-second exposures allowed to view it.

The control subjects neither recognized nor recalled any of the matrices. As in Experiment 2, our attempt to use savings scores as a retention measure was not useful. When savings scores were calculated for individual matrices, all subjects (including Rajan) produced both positive and negative savings scores under both the 12-month and 6-month retention intervals.

Experiment 4: Fourteen-Month Retention

Because Rajan had shown substantial forgetting over 6 months with a test that we assumed was unexpected, we decided to examine forgetting with a shorter retention interval. Thus, we administered another unexpected retention test 2 months after the test just described. The control subjects were completing another experiment and were not available for this study.

There were 30 matrices in this retention test. Six of the matrices were from Matrix Set One (the remaining untested matrices), 12 were from Matrix Set Three (the new matrices in that set), and 12 were new. The pattern of repetition of matrices is shown in Table 4.2. Again, the procedure for learning the matrices was identical to that used in Experiment 2.

Recognition and Recall Data. After a 14-month retention interval, Rajan recognized all 6 of the matrices from Matrix Set One with no false alarms. He was able to give the identifying number for 2 of those matrices. In addition, he correctly recalled one 5 × 5 matrix from Matrix Set One. As we indicated earlier, given Rajan's facility for rapid learning, this performance may have reflected study during the two 10-second exposure times rather than recall.

His performance on the 2-month-old matrices was fairly consistent with his performance on the 6-month-old items in the previous experiment. He correctly identified 7 of the 12 matrices with five false alarms. He could not give the identifying number (within the set) for any of the matrices. Further, he misidentified all seven regarding when he had learned them (i.e., he placed them all as having been presented more than 2 months earlier). Finally, he was not able to recall any of the matrices.

Conclusions on Retention of Matrices

We think that the evidence from our measures of Rajan's retention provides reasonable support for three conclusions. First, we think that his performance on the initial matrices shows that he can maintain outstanding performance on number sets with some rehearsal. Given Rajan's general approach to study, we speculate that the rehearsal was minimal and unsystematic. His recognition performance remained essentially perfect over 14 months and his ability to recall 8 of 12 matrices at 6 months was also impressive. However, the fact that he could not show equally impressive performance on retention tests for Matrix Set Two suggests, we believe, that he had not rehearsed that matrix set.

That interpretation is also supported by the observation that he was unable to recall any of the matrices from Matrix Set One after 1 year even though he recalled some of the Minnesota matrices after 8½ years. The entire pattern of performance suggests that his long-term retention of some of the matrices in our initial study as well as some of the Minnesota matrices resulted from rehearsal of those matrices.

Second, we believe that Rajan had not anticipated retention tests on the new matrices in the second and third matrix sets, and that his performance on those sets represents a test of his memory unaided by rehearsal. Those tests show that he cannot recall matrices after a retention intervals of 2 or 6 months unless they have been rehearsed. However, his ability to recognize matrices is good. He was able to recognize roughly two-thirds of the matrices at both retention intervals. That performance is substantially above that of the control subjects.

Third, the pattern of data also supports our contention that Rajan did not physically record the matrices. If he had recorded them, his performance at 1 year could have been as "good" as his performance at 6 months. Indeed, he could have shown "perfect performance" at any retention interval. Rajan has a strong desire to look good on these tests, but we are quite confident that this does not extend to recording the matrices. We repeat that nothing we observed in Rajan's study or personal habits suggested he was either compulsive or systematic in keeping any kinds of records. In addition, we never saw any evidence that he recorded any of the test material.

Rajan's memory over long retention intervals is clearly not as spectacular as the memory reported for Shereshevskii (Luria, 1968) and documented for VP

(Hunt & Love, 1972). At the same time, his memory performance on matrices is substantially superior to well-practiced control subjects.

TESTING THE PAIRED-ASSOCIATE HYPOTHESIS

Rajan obviously is extremely skilled at learning strings of numbers including number matrices. As we noted in chapter 1, it is that very skill which makes his strategy for learning the strings difficult to discern. However, even a skilled performer provides clues as to the strategies involved in the skill (e.g., studies of chess skill such as Chase & Simon, 1973). We designed our experiments to unearth such clues and searched for clues from other experiments.

The memory span experiments described in chapter 2 suggested that Rajan kept track of the location of sequences within the span. (Note that we use location to refer to the serial position of digits within the memory span or within a row of digits in a matrix.) As indicated in Table 2.1, when Rajan gave partial information (a portion of a span), he almost always was correct on the location of that sequence within the span. We note that he typically volunteered location information whether or not he was asked for it.

The evidence from the initial matrix study (Experiment 1) also seemed to point to the importance of location information for Rajan. Furthermore, he treated a row of a matrix as a chunk; rather than grouping the digits in a row into smaller chunks, he appeared to keep track of the location of each digit in that row. That is, he seemed to know that the digit in Column 5 of Row 4 is 2, the digit in Column 3 of Row 6 is 8, and so on. In short, he appeared to be learning location–digit pairs. As we have noted, this procedure is called paired-associate learning in the learning literature.

Rajan's use of a paired-associate procedure to learn the matrices is interesting. The use of location–digit pairs would seem to be very cumbersome and, more importantly, virtually devoid of meaning. In contrast, most individuals usually increase the use of some sort of meaningful chunking procedure to retain information as they become more skilled. For example, skilled chess players group the pieces on the board into meaningful groups, whereas novice chess players do not. Chunking allows an expert chess player to reproduce about four times as many pieces on a chess board from memory as a novice (e.g., Chase & Simon, 1973). It is rather surprising that Rajan does not appear to create meaningful subsets of the material.

If we begin with the strong assumption that Rajan is using *only* the paired-associate procedure for learning the rows of a matrix, one prediction is quite clear. Specifically, with pure paired-associate learning, it should make little difference how the digits are presented during study providing that the location within the row (and the location of the row) is clearly identified for each digit.

Thus, if the digits were presented one at a time with the location of the digits clearly identified, it should make little difference whether the matrix is presented in serial order or in a random order.[1] When a random order is used, there probably would be some additional time used in determining the location of each digit (e.g., this digit is in the third column of the fifth row). However, that time should be minimal when the location is clearly marked. Thus, the time taken to learn the matrix should be nearly the same under both conditions.

Two experiments were conducted to test the prediction outlined before. Rajan was the only subject in these experiments.

Experiment 5: Random Presentation with Asterisks

This experiment was designed to test the prediction that the manner in which a matrix is presented to Rajan should not make much difference if he is given the location of the digits within the matrix. Because the presentation procedure was quite different from that used previously, we also were interested in determining whether Rajan would speed up as he learned successive sets of matrices as Chase and Ericsson (e.g., 1981, 1982) would predict. Finally, we expected to see the list length effect in both conditions with the larger matrices taking more time per digit to learn.

Rajan was given a series of 60 matrices with half presented serially and half presented randomly. The order of presentation of matrix type (serial or random) was random. Five matrices of each of six sizes (3×3, 4×4, 5×5, 7×7, 9×9, and 10×10) were used for each presentation condition. During presentation, each matrix was outlined on the computer screen as a square array of boxes. For example, a 10×10 matrix was shown as 100 boxes in a 10×10 array.

Presentation of the matrix began with a digit appearing in one of the boxes. Rajan studied the digit as long as he wished and then advanced to the next digit by pressing the spacebar. The digit just studied disappeared to be replaced by an asterisk while the next digit appeared in another box. Under serial presentation, the digits appeared in normal reading order starting with the upper left-hand corner of the matrix. In contrast, the location of the digits under random presentation was determined by sampling the locations randomly without replacement. The computer was programmed to record the study time for each digit. When Rajan completed study of the matrix, he was required to recall the matrix as a serial matrix whether the presentation order was serial or random. His time to recall the matrix as well as the number and location of any errors were recorded.

There was one deviation from the presentation sequence just described. The second time Rajan was given a 10×10 matrix under the random presentation condition, he announced that he had completely lost the matrix when he attempted recall. He was very disturbed by his inability to retrieve the matrix and asked

---

[1]We wish to thank Richard Shiffrin for suggesting this analytic manipulation to us.

to be given another 10 × 10 matrix in its place. We accommodated him during the next test session and he reproduced that matrix without error. It was the only 10 × 10 matrix that he recalled without error in the random presentation condition. We note that he took 26 seconds per digit to study the matrix that he was unable to reproduce, whereas he took 22 seconds per digit to study the matrix that he recalled without error.

Overall Performance

Rate of Learning. There was a large difference in the mean time per digit to learn the matrices under the serial (3.7 seconds) and random (16.1 seconds) presentation conditions.

Error Data. Rajan rarely makes errors in recall of a matrix when the whole matrix is provided for study. Thus, the error data for both serial and random presentation stand in sharp contrast to error data for whole matrix presentation.

In the serial presentation condition, Rajan made no errors on the 3 × 3, 4 × 4, and 5 × 5 matrices. He recalled three of five matrices without error in each of the other three sets. He made one error on one 7 × 7 matrix and two errors on another 7 × 7 matrix. He made three errors on one 9 × 9 matrix and 37 errors on another 9 × 9 matrix. In the 10 × 10 matrix set, he made five errors on one matrix and 21 errors on another. Overall, Rajan recalled 80% of the serially presented matrices without error.

The number of errorless matrices was reduced in the random presentation condition. Rajan recalled all of the 3 × 3 matrices without error and was errorless in three of the five matrices for the 4 × 4, 5 × 5, and 7 × 7 matrix sets. He also recalled one 9 × 9 matrix and one 10 × 10 matrix without error. With the exception of one 9 × 9 matrix with 33 errors, the number of errors per matrix ranged from one to five. In summary, Rajan recalled 53% of the randomly presented matrices without error.

The error data demonstrate that the longer study times per digit in the larger matrices do not reflect any speed–accuracy tradeoff. That is, both his speed and his accuracy decreased in the larger matrices.

We should also note that Rajan had a strong desire to perform perfectly on these matrices. We are convinced that the three matrices on which Rajan made a large number of errors were matrices on which he lost the location of one or more digits and gave up in disgust. It was difficult to convince Rajan to keep trying when, in his eyes, he had failed.

List Length Effects

As noted in the introduction to this experiment, we expected to see the usual list length effect under both conditions. That is, the time per digit to learn a matrix should increase as the size of the matrix increases. That effect occurred as ex-

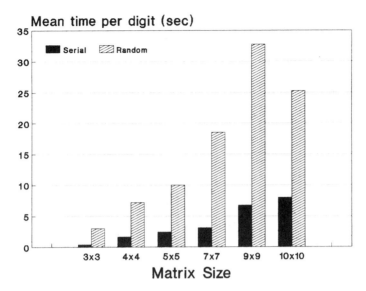

FIG. 4.4.   Mean time per digit to learn a matrix as a function of matrix size presented separately for serial and random presentation. These data are from matrices
in which asterisks replaced each digit after presentation.

pected and is shown in Fig. 4.4. The inversion of the effect for the two largest
matrices in the random condition reflects, in our opinion, the instability of the
data owing to the small number of matrices in each set.

Practice Effects

Because this was a new procedure for Rajan, we expected to see his performance speed up with practice. The relevant data are presented in Fig. 4.5. As can
be seen, his performance did speed up under the random condition but did not
under the serial condition. Apparently, the serial condition was similar enough
to whole presentation (with which he had ample practice) to preclude any increase
in speed of performance under that condition.

Comparison with Whole-Matrix Presentation

Because four of the matrix sizes (5 × 5, 7 × 7, 9 × 9, and 10 × 10) are
the same as those used in the original matrix study (Experiment 1), we can make
a rough comparison of performance under conditions when the entire matrix is
available for study and when the digits are presented singly in serial order. The
mean time to learn each matrix size under the two conditions is presented in Table 4.4. Using the comparable matrices, the overall mean time per digit to learn
the matrix when the entire matrix is available is 2.4 seconds. By comparison,
the comparable time per digit for the serial condition was 5.1 seconds. Thus,

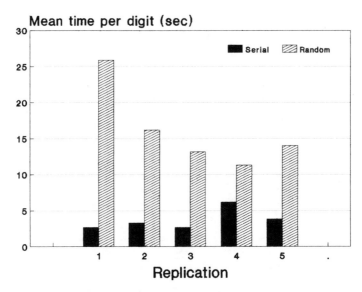

FIG. 4.5. Mean time per digit to learn each set of matrices presented separately for serial and random presentation. These data are from matrices in which asterisks replaced each digit after presentation.

there is an additional and substantial benefit to presenting the matrix as a complete set. Note, however, that he *can* learn a matrix even under the random condition. Particularly for the larger matrices (9 × 9 and 10 × 10), that is an impressive performance.

Estimating the Time Taken to Locate Each Digit

We noted in the introduction to this section that when random presentation is used there would be some additional time used in determining the location of each digit (e.g., this digit is in the third column of the fifth row). It is possible

TABLE 4.4
Mean Time Per Digit to Learn Each Matrix Size Presented Separately for
Whole-Matrix Presentation (Experiment 1) and Serial Presentation (Experiment 5)

	Matrix Size			
	5 × 5	7 × 7	9 × 9	10 × 10
Whole-matrix Presentation (Experiment 1)	2.1	1.7	2.7	3.1
Serial Presentation (Experiment 5)	2.5	3.1	6.7	8.0

that the difference between serial and random presentation could be accounted for by that location time.

We investigated that possibility by deriving an estimate of the mean time taken to determine the location within the matrix of each presented digit (hereafter called *location time*). We decided to use a conservative estimate of location time as a starting point.

For each matrix, we ordered the study times and ignored the fastest N times where N corresponded to the row length in the matrix (i.e., N was 3 for a 3 × 3 matrix, 4 for a 4 × 4 matrix, etc.). Then we took the mean of the next N fastest times as the uncorrected location time for that matrix. Finally, we averaged these means to obtain our estimate of uncorrected location time for each matrix size.

We used this procedure to derive uncorrected location times because all matrices included some very fast times. We believe that those rapid times represent cases in which Rajan simply read the presented digit and went on to the next digit. Either he was immediately able to identify location or was able to retroactively identify the location.

The uncorrected mean location time must overestimate location time because it includes the time to read digits. The estimate does not necessarily include rehearsal time because Rajan would often read two or three digits rather quickly and then pause to rehearse them.

To get an estimate of reading time, we used the serially presented 3 × 3 matrices. A 3 × 3 matrix is well within Rajan's memory span. He went through those matrices very rapidly but paused briefly after the last digit before he recited them. Thus, we used the mean study time for those matrices, excluding the last digit, as an estimate of reading time. That estimate was .38 seconds.

We subtracted .38 seconds from the uncorrected mean location times as our final estimate of mean location time. The resulting mean location times were 2.44, 4.02, 3.81, 5.04, 6.54, and 5.91 seconds for the 3 × 3, 4 × 4, 5 × 5, 7 × 7, 9 × 9, and 10 × 10 matrices, respectively. Over all random matrices, the mean location time was 4.63 seconds.

Most importantly, it is obvious that the overall location time of approximately 4.6 seconds cannot account for the 12 second time-per-digit difference in matrix learning between serial and random presentation. Similarly, subtracting location times does not modify our conclusions about list length effects. Finally, note that inspection of those mean location times suggests that there is an increase in location time with an increase in matrix size.

Experiment 6: Random Presentation Without Asterisks

One might reasonably expect location time to increase with an increase in matrix size. However, midway through the experiment, Rajan pointed out that the asterisks served as place holders for the numbers so that he had only had to determine the row in which the digit appeared in the random condition. That is, he could remember a sequence of digits for a given row (e.g., the digits 483 have appeared at locations 2,5, and 8 in row 7) and then modify the series by inserting the new digit in the appropriate place in that sequence (e.g., if 9 is shown at Location 6, the sequence is changed to 4893). Given that information, the magnitude of the difference in difficulty between the 3 × 3 and 10 × 10 matrices might well be masked by the information provided by the asterisks.

Obviously, our attempt to force Rajan to use only the location in the matrix of each digit as an identifier was flawed. We were interested in establishing whether Rajan was capable of learning a matrix when *only* location information was provided. In the present experiment, we presented the digits singly as before but left no asterisk to mark their location following presentation.

As in the previous experiment, Rajan was given a total of 60 matrices with half presented serially and half presented randomly. The order of presentation of matrix type (serial or random) was random. Five matrices of each of six sizes (3 × 3, 4 × 4, 5 × 5, 7 × 7, 9 × 9, and 10 × 10) were used for each presentation condition. The procedure was identical to that used in the previous experiment except that asterisks were not used to mark previously presented digits. As before, the computer was programmed to record the study time for each digit. When Rajan completed study of the matrix, his time to recall the matrix as well as the number and location of any errors was recorded.

We modified the procedure in another important way by requiring Rajan to meet a performance criterion during recall. We had two reasons for the modification. First, we wanted his performance during recall to be roughly equivalent to the prior experiment. That is, we wanted to equate performance observed when the asterisks were absent to performance observed when the asterisks were present as place markers. Second, Rajan appeared to be getting bored with this type of experiment. That was not surprising because, up to this point, he had been required to learn over 140 unique matrices ranging in size from 3 × 3 to 20 × 20. In part, the performance criteria was adopted as a counter to our perception of Rajan's drop in motivation.

The performance criterion varied with the type of matrix. We required Rajan to recall the smaller matrices (3 × 3, 4 × 4, and 5 × 5) without error. He was allowed to make errors on the larger matrices, but a criterion of no more than 5% errors had to be met. If Rajan failed to meet the criterion for a matrix, he was retested on a new matrix of the same size. With this criterion, Rajan was required to repeat five serial matrices (one 4 × 4, one 5 × 5, and three 9 × 9) and seven random matrices (three 7 × 7, three 9 × 9, and one 10 × 10). In addition, experimenter error made it necessary to repeat two 10 × 10 matrices (one serial, one random).

Overall Performance.   In the following analyses, the data from matrices meeting the error criteria are used. There was a large difference in the mean time per digit to learn the matrices under the serial (2.4 seconds) and random (14.7

seconds) presentation conditions. These data show again that Rajan benefits from having information other than the location of each digit within a matrix.

Although Rajan claimed that learning matrices without the asterisks as place holders was a much more difficult task than when the asterisks were present, these data do not support his contention. On the matrices he mastered, his performance without asterisks is quite comparable to performance with asterisks. Obviously, we can draw no firm conclusions because he had additional practice on this most difficult task. Nonetheless, the asterisks seem irrelevant in the serial condition and the data are consistent with that conjecture. Similarly, the asterisks might have been helpful in the random condition, and the data suggest the possibility of only a very modest facilitative effect of the asterisks.

List Length Effects. Again, we expected to see the usual list length effect under both conditions. That is, the time per digit to learn a matrix should increase as the size of the matrix increases. That effect occurred as expected and is shown in Fig. 4.6. There is a systematic increase in time per digit as the size of the matrix increases, and that increase occurs under both conditions.

Practice Effects. Because this procedure could be viewed as yet another new procedure for Rajan, it seemed possible that we might expect to see his performance speed up with practice. The relevant data are presented in Fig. 4.7. As can be seen, there is a suggestion that his performance did speed up under

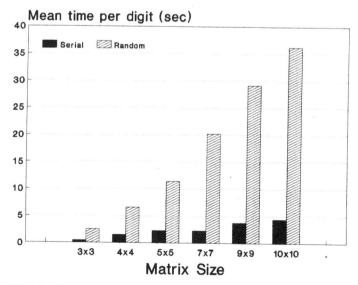

FIG. 4.6.   Mean time per digit to learn a matrix as a function of matrix size presented separately for serial and random presentation. These data are from matrices in which asterisks did not replace each digit after presentation.

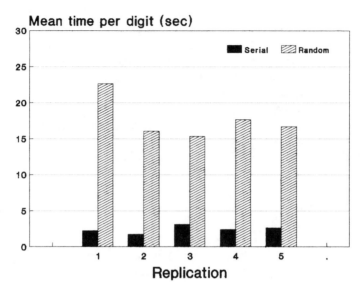

FIG. 4.7.   Mean time per digit to learn each set of matrices presented separately for serial and random presentation. These data are from matrices in which asterisks did not replace each digit after presentation.

the random condition, but there is no evidence for speed-up under the serial condition. That pattern of data fits our view that the asterisks were irrelevant for serial presentation of the matrix but were useful when the matrix was presented randomly.

Estimating the Time Taken to Locate Each Digit.   As in the previous experiment, we derived an estimate of the mean location times for each matrix size. We used the same procedure as the previous experiment. We began by using the serially presented 3 × 3 matrices to get an estimate of reading time. That estimate was .30 seconds.

As before, we subtracted .30 seconds from the mean uncorrected location times as our final estimate of the mean location times. The resulting mean location times are shown in Fig. 4.8. Consistent with the data for presentation with asterisks, these data show a steadily increasing mean time to determine the location of the digit within the matrix as matrix size increases. The overall mean location time was 5.89 seconds.

Once again, the most important finding is that the overall location time of approximately 6 seconds does not begin to account for the 12-second time-per-digit difference in matrix learning under serial and random presentation. These data clearly demonstrate that Rajan must be using something other than, or in addition to, a paired-associate learning procedure with location as the cue and the digit at that location as the target.

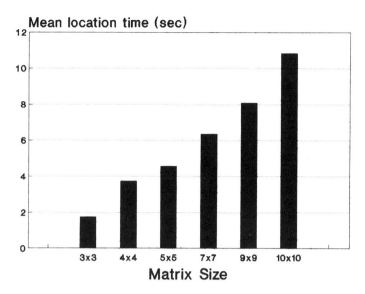

FIG. 4.8. Mean time taken to locate each digit presented separately for each matrix size.

CONCLUSIONS

Visual Imagery

Rajan has repeatedly stated that his performance with digits does not depend on visual imagery. All of our evidence, together with evidence from other laboratories strongly supports the conclusion that he is absolutely correct. The experiments with matrices in this chapter showed clearly that he does not read the matrices from a visual image when recalled. If he did, time for recall of rows and columns from a matrix would be essentially equivalent. In fact, he takes far longer to recall columns than to recall rows.

We noted in chapter 3 that our tests showed that his recall of complex figures was unexceptional. We also noted that other investigators showed that his performance on a spatial memory task was lower than that of eight control subjects (Biederman, Cooper, Fox, & Mahadevan, 1992). In yet another series of tests, his visual performance was also poor relative to control subjects (Baddeley, Mahadevan, & Thompson, 1992).

Taken together, these data support the conclusion put forth in the psychometric profile—Rajan is, at best, average on visual tasks and probably has a deficit in visual imagery.

Encoding Strategy

These data also show that Rajan can learn relatively difficult matrices when only location information is available. That is, he is capable of using a paired-associate strategy (i.e., pairing the digits with their locations) to learn and reproduce a matrix of digits. At the same time, Rajan performs better when the digits in the matrix are presented in serial order rather than in a random order. He also performs better when he has the whole matrix available for study compared to serial presentation of single digits.

The difference between serial presentation and whole-matrix presentation is not very analytic. There are obvious advantages to having the whole matrix available for study which do not preclude the use of a paired-associate procedure as the primary learning strategy. For example, Rajan could go through the matrix very quickly and then use a self-testing procedure to determine whether he had all parts of the matrix available for recall. With the entire matrix available, he could do further study on digits that were not available or difficult to retrieve. That sort of study–test–study procedure should become extremely efficient with practice.

The difference between serial and random presentation of the digits in the matrix provides more useful information. If Rajan is using a paired-associate procedure for learning the digits, one would expect a difference between serial and random presentation based on the difficulty of establishing each location. That is, Rajan must establish the location of a digit within a matrix in order to pair that location with the digit. That task should be fairly trivial when the digits are presented in serial order. The task becomes more difficult when the digits are presented in random order. As described earlier, we attempted to estimate the time to determine the location of a digit within a matrix. The critical data are in the experiment where the digits were presented without asterisks marking their location. The estimated mean location time of 6 seconds (over all matrices) is well short of the overall 12-second time-per-digit difference in matrix learning under serial and random presentation. We have noted that those data demonstrate that Rajan must be using something other than, or in addition to, a paired-associate learning procedure with location as the cue and the digit at that location as the target.

Given the consistency with which Rajan identifies location in both memory span and matrix learning studies, we conclude that he uses a paired-associate procedure in addition to learning strings of digits by rote. It is possible that he attaches meaning to those strings but it seems unlikely given his failure to attempt to attach meaning in other situations (such as the word–list study). As we noted earlier, Rajan appears to focus on the location of a sequence (in the span or matrix) and essentially learns the sequence by rote. We reiterate that rote learning of a series of digits is a very difficult task and we are surprised to find no evidence for any consistent effort to attach meaning to strings of numbers. Rajan keeps track of the location of those strings in the span or matrix.

CHAPTER 5

Memory Search

The primary purpose of this chapter is to produce an account of how Rajan conducts a memory search on a large set of numbers. The numbers used here are the first 10,000 decimal digits of pi. We focus on the first 10,000 digits because they have been extremely well learned by Rajan.

We present two sets of experiments in this chapter that focus on two different problems, and we follow each set of experiments with a discussion of the information gleaned from them. In the first set of three experiments, we looked at searches to retrieve single digits from specific locations (e.g., the 4,782nd decimal digit of pi). Those experiments confirmed Rajan's description of his strategy for retrieval. In the second set of three experiments, we had Rajan find sequences of digits at unknown locations. As will be seen, the searches for sequences showed how Rajan has the digits of pi organized in memory.

SEARCHING FOR DIGITS AT SPECIFIC LOCATIONS

Experiment 1: Digit Location

We began these investigations with a few informal tests in which we asked Rajan to retrieve digits from specific locations in pi (e.g., the 8,347th decimal digit of pi). It quickly became obvious that Rajan could perform this task with reasonable accuracy. His retrieval times varied from 3 to 30 seconds but did not appear to vary systematically with location in the 10,000-digit series.

Rajan's memory search appeared to be organized in a manner which reflected the organization of the source from which he learned the digits, a reproduction

75

of a paper by Shanks and Wrench (1962). In that paper, the authors computed and presented the first 100,000 digits of pi. A reproduction of one of the pages of the digits is shown as Fig. 5.1. As can be seen, each page contains 5,000 digits. The digits are grouped in 10-digit strings with 10 such strings, hence, 100 digits, in a row. The rows are also grouped in 10-row blocks to produce a block of 1,000 digits. As just noted, there were five such blocks on a page.

When we asked Rajan to describe his memory search, he claimed that he quickly located the correct row (of 100 digits) and then counted across the row to locate the correct digit. If his introspective report were correct, the search time to locate digits should vary substantially with location in a row (but not with location of the row) in the 10,000 digit series.

Method

The method for the first three experiments was very similar. Thus, we give a complete description here and only note variations from the method in the next two experiments.

The materials on which Rajan was tested were the first 10,000 decimal digits of pi taken from Shanks and Wrench (1962). A computer program was created

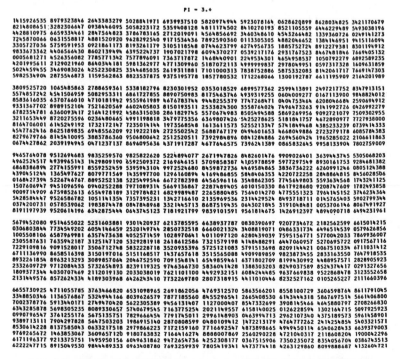

FIG. 5.1. Reprinted from "Computation of pi to 100,000 decimals," by Daniel Shanks and John W. Wrench, Jr., *Mathematics of Computation, Volume 16*, by permission of the American Mathematical Society.

to sample 2,000 digit locations from the first 10,000 digits of pi. The 10,000 locations were divided into blocks of five (i.e., locations 1–5, 6–10, 11–15, etc.), and one location was randomly sampled from each of the 5-digit blocks. The resulting 2,000 locations were then randomized for presentation in the search task.

Rajan was seated facing a computer monitor. The experimenter both initiated and terminated a trial by pressing the spacebar. Experimenter control was used so that Rajan would not terminate the trial in anticipation of locating the target digit. When Rajan said he was ready, the trial number (e.g., Trial #9) and the target location (e.g., 4,782) were presented one above the other in the center of the screen. The trial was terminated when he called out the target digit. The experimenter had a printout containing the trial number, target digit location, and target digit to verify the accuracy of the search. When Rajan made an error, we asked him to give the string of 10 digits from which he had taken the (erroneous) target digit. That procedure enabled us to analyze his errors. The trial number, target location, response time, and accuracy (correct or incorrect target digit) of the search were recorded.

Searches proceeded at a rate dictated by Rajan. The search task rarely continued for more than one hour. When it did, a minimum 10-minute break was given after the first hour.

Results

We tabulated Rajan's error rate over trials, the types of errors made, the median search time for correct and incorrect searches, and median search time for each component location (e.g., 100-digit row within each 1,000-digit block).

Error Rate. Rajan began this task with a very high error rate (20% in the first 100 trials) but showed a rapid reduction in error rate over the first 500 trials. His error rate for the last 1,000 trials was reduced to 1.0%. His overall error rate for the 2,000 trials was 4.2%.

Error Type. When Rajan made an error, we had him give us the string of 10 digits from which he had given the erroneous target digit. With that information, we were able to determine that most of Rajan's search errors clearly were not random. Of his total of 83 errors, we identified 52 counting errors. We assumed that he made a counting error under the following three conditions: (a) The digit was in the right location within the string and the string was in the right location within a row of 100 digits, but it was in the preceding or following row (20 such errors); (b) the digit was in the right location within the string, but the string either immediately followed or immediately preceded the correct target string (18 such errors); or (c) the digit was is the correct target string but either preceded or followed the target digit (14 such errors).

In addition, he made one error that was exactly 1,000 digits in error (1,000 block counting error) and another error that was exactly 5,000 digits in error (i.e., correct location, wrong page). On eight other occasions, he recited the correct 10-digit target string but selected the wrong digit for unknown reasons. There were five cases in which Rajan gave us the correct target string of 10 digits with an error at the target location.

The remaining 16 errors appeared to be completely unsystematic. There were two instances on which he became confused and did not give a target string. In eight cases, we located the sequence Rajan gave us, but his error did not appear to be systematic. There were only six instances for which we could not find the sequence which he produced as the target string.

In summary, Rajan was exceptionally accurate at this task. Approximately 65% of his errors were counting errors, and in another 10% of the cases, he gave the correct 10-digit string and correct location within the string but recalled the wrong digit at that location.

Median Search Times for Correct and Incorrect Responses.   Rajan's median search time for incorrect responses was 14.9 seconds. His median search time for correct responses was 13.0 seconds. His median search time speeded up somewhat with practice and was 11.6 seconds on the last 1,000 trials.

Median Search Times by Location.   Rajan claimed that he went rapidly to the correct row of 100 digits and then counted across the row to locate the correct digit. If that is correct, his response times should show a substantial systematic change dependent on the location of the target digit within the row. By contrast, search time for rows should show little change with the location of the row in the 10,000-digit sequence.

In order to consider the effect of digit location within a row as well as the effect of the location of the row in the overall sequence, we collapsed the data to obtain median search times for blocks of 25 rows (i.e., 2,500 digits) and for 20-digit blocks within each row. Errors were excluded from the calculations. The medians for those data are shown in Fig. 5.2. As can be seen, there was a large systematic increase in search time as the location within the row increased. The first 20 digits were the best estimate for the time it took Rajan to find a given row. Search time for the first 20 digits changed only slightly with location of the row in the 10,000-digit set.

However, an increase in search time as the location of the row increases is not analytic because the increase could be attributed either to increased time to locate the row or to increased time to search through the row, or both. Because these data were inconclusive, we decided to perform a direct test of Rajan's speed at locating specific rows.

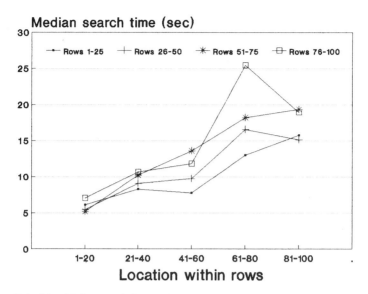

FIG. 5.2.   Median search times to locate specific digits within the first 10,000 digits of pi.

Experiment 2: Row Location

Rajan claimed that he quickly located the appropriate row when doing a memory search for a target digit. To test his claim directly, we presented Rajan with target locations beginning each of the 100 rows in the first 10,000 decimal digits of pi (e.g., locations such as 6,901, 301, 2,701, which are the locations of the first digit in rows 70, 4, and 28, respectively). His task was to recite the target row as rapidly as possible.

Method

As printed in the source, there are 100 rows (of 100 digits) in the first 10,000 decimal digits of pi. We generated the set of locations which began each of the 100 rows (i.e., 1, 101, 201, 301, etc.). We then performed 10 separate randomizations of these locations and concatenated them to form a total set of 1,000 target locations.

The procedure was very similar to that used in Experiment 1 except that Rajan was required to recite the appropriate row and his time to recite the row was recorded. Thus, on each trial the target location, response accuracy (correct or incorrect), response time (to begin recitation), and recitation time were recorded.

Results

We tabulated Rajan's error rate over trials (an error was recorded if Rajan incorrectly recited any of the first five digits), his distribution of search times (i.e., time to locate a row), his median search time by location (e.g., row within 1,000 blocks), and the time to recite a row-by-row location.

Error Rate.   Unlike his error rate in the previous experiment, Rajan's error rate did not vary systematically over trials. His mean error rate overall was 3.1%. When tabulated by 100 trial blocks, his error rate varied between 1% and 6%.

Median Search Times for Correct and Incorrect Responses.   Rajan's median search time for incorrect responses was 2.1 seconds. His median search time for correct responses was 1.5 seconds. The search times included the reaction time of the experimenter to hit the key as well as Rajan's time for encoding and production. Obviously, Rajan's report about his strategy in searching memory for a digit location was supported in at least one respect. He could get to the correct row very rapidly during a memory search.

Median Search Time to Locate Rows.   To determine whether Rajan's response time to locate rows varied systematically by row location, we tabulated the response times by 10-row block (i.e., 1,000-digit block). Errors were excluded from the calculations. The median response time for each 10-row block is given in Table 5.1. As can be seen, the response time varied modestly, if at all, with location of the 1,000 block in the 10,000 digit set.

TABLE 5.1
Median Response Time to Locate a Row in Seconds.
The Data are Grouped by 10-Row Block (1,000 Block)

1000 Block		
Block #	*Mean RT*	*Observations*
1	1.4	89
2	1.5	98
3	1.6	99
4	1.5	95
5	1.6	98
6	1.5	92
7	1.5	98
8	1.6	96
9	1.8	96
10	1.6	98

Median Row Recitation Time.   To determine whether Rajan's time to re-cite a row varied systematically by row location, we tabulated the row recitation times by five-row block. The median row recitation time for each five-row block is given in Fig. 5.3. As can be seen, the row recitation time increased only slightly over the first 5,000 digits but increased substantially during the second 5,000 digits.

Discussion

Rajan's median search time to locate a row taken together with his median recitation time for a row strongly support his description of his procedure for locating a specific digit of pi. His median search time to locate a correct row was 1.5 seconds, whereas his median search time to locate correctly a specific digit was 13.0 seconds. It is clear, therefore, that most of his time was spent searching for the correct digit within the row. Furthermore, consider that the median row location time included experimenter reaction time and Rajan's en-coding/production time. While Rajan's claim that he located the row "almost im-mediately" may be hyperbole, he certainly was very fast.

These data also show that row recitation time at best increased only slightly over the first 5,000 digits but increased substantially during the second 5,000 digits. We believe that difference can be attributed to differences in degree of learning. Rajan learned the digits of pi in a sequential manner that involved

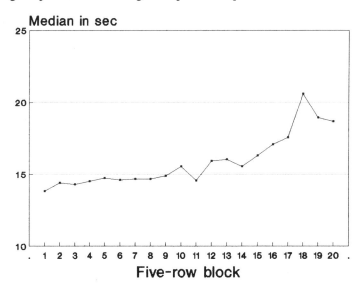

FIG. 5.3.   Median time to recite a row by blocks of five rows. The data are from Rajan.

rehearsing previously learned blocks of pi (the usual block is 1,000 digits) to ensure that the entire set was correctly mastered. That procedure guarantees that prior blocks of digits will be better learned (or overlearned) relative to subsequent blocks. Further, Rajan uses the page on which the first 5,000 digits of pi are printed whenever he exhibits his knowledge of pi. Those occasions are sufficiently numerous to produce considerable additional practice on the first 5,000 digits.

Finally, these data strongly suggest that the increase in search time over blocks of rows found in the previous experiment represents increasing time to locate the digit within a row rather than increasing time to locate a row.

Experiment 3: Locating Digits Within a Row

The row location data from the previous experiment demonstrated that Rajan could get to the appropriate row very quickly. At the same time, the row recitation data also suggested that his time to locate a target digit varied both with location in the row and location in the 10,000-digit series. To further examine his time to locate a target digit within a row, we used a procedure which allowed Rajan to locate the target row before he was given the target location within the row. Using that procedure, Rajan was presented with target locations selected from each of the 100 rows in the first 10,000 decimal digits of pi.

Method

Four target locations were randomly selected for each of the 100 rows (of 100 digits) from the following locations within the row: 11–30, 31–50, 51–70, and 71–90, respectively. We omitted the first and last 10 digits from consideration because we believed Rajan might have rapid access to those 10-digit strings. The selected locations were randomized to produce a total set of 400 target locations.

The procedure was similar to that used in Experiment 2 except that Rajan was given the target row first (e.g., "The target will be in row 70"). The target location (e.g., 6,947) was presented only after Rajan indicated that he had located the correct row. On each trial, the target location, response accuracy (correct or incorrect), and response time (to locate the target digit within the row) were recorded.

Results

We tabulated Rajan's error rate over trials, his distribution of search times within a row, and his median search time by location (e.g., digit within a row).

Error Rate. Rajan began with a relatively high error rate for the first 100 trials (6%) but reduced his error rate to zero on the last 100 trials. His overall error rate was 2.5%.

Median Search Times for Correct and Incorrect Responses. Rajan's median search time for incorrect responses was 32.3 seconds. His median search time for correct responses was 8.3 seconds. These data show that, when he was correct, Rajan found a digit within a row rather quickly. However, his median time to find a digit within a row was more than five times as long as his median time to locate a row.

Median Search Times by Row Location. We divided the 10,000 locations into four successive blocks of 2,500 digits each. Then we calculated the median search time for each of four blocks of locations within a row (i.e., locations 10–29, 30–49, 50–69, and 70–89) separately for each block of 2,500 digits. Because errors were excluded from the calculations, the number of search times from which the median were calculated ranged between 23 and 25. These median search times are presented in Fig. 5.4. As can be seen, Rajan's time to locate a target digit increased systematically as the location in the row increased. His search time also increased over blocks of 2,500 digits. That increase was particularly marked for the last 2,500 digits in the series.

Conclusion

These data remove the ambiguity from the results found in Experiment 1. It took longer to locate a digit within a row in the last 25 (of 100) rows than to locate a digit in the same place in the first 25 rows. However, these search times

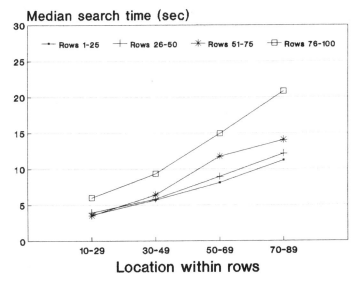

FIG. 5.4.   Median search times to locate specific digits within the first 10,000 digits of pi with the row given prior to the start of the search.

do not include location of the row because the row was found before the target location was given. Thus, the increased time must be attributed to increased time to search through the row (in later rows) rather than increased time to find the row.

Rajan's Retrieval Strategy

The three experiments on digit location tell us a great deal about how Rajan has the first 10,000 digits of pi encoded for subsequent retrieval. The data clearly demonstrate that he has them encoded for retrieval by row (of 100 digits) as printed on the source sheets. The error data in the first experiment also strongly suggests that he has the rows encoded in chunks of 10 digits. The procedure for locating the errors required that he give us the string (as printed on the source sheets) of 10 digits from which he retrieved the erroneous digit – he was able to do that quickly and easily. More importantly, over two-thirds (i.e., 57 of 83) of his errors were errors in which he either made a counting error or a retrieval error. In the case of counting errors, he gave a digit in the correct location within a string of 10 digits but was in error either by one digit, one string within the row, or one row. In the case of retrieval errors, he gave all other digits within the string correctly but erred on the target digit.

Taken together, the three experiments confirm Rajan's contention that he found the row in which the target digit was located rather swiftly and then essentially counted over to the target digit. The time to locate the target digit increased with location in the row and location of the row in the overall series. The latter increase is attributable to the time it took to find the digit within the last 25 rows and not to the time it took to find the row.

We can attribute, with considerable confidence, the increase in search time over the series to differences in degree of learning. As we noted earlier, Rajan learned the digits of pi in a manner that guaranteed prior blocks of digits will be better learned (or overlearned) relative to subsequent blocks. He also uses the page on which the first 5,000 digits of pi are printed for demonstrations. Those demonstrations occur frequently and therefore produce considerable additional practice on the first 5,000 digits.

SEARCHING FOR SEQUENCES: EVIDENCE FOR CHUNKING

Experiment 4: Ten-Digit Strings

Rajan's errors in searching for target digits at a specific location (Experiment 1) suggested that he has the digits chunked in strings of 10 as printed in the source from which he learned the digits. If that hypothesis is correct, Rajan should be able to locate a sequence of 10 digits taken from pi relatively quickly if the sequence corresponds to a printed string. Furthermore, his search should take much longer if the 10-digit target sequence spans two successive printed strings (e.g., starts at the fourth digit within a printed string). Hereafter, we will use the terms *complete string* and *spanning string* to refer to the two types of sequences just described. In this experiment, we had Rajan locate both complete and spanning strings to determine whether his encoded chunks correspond to the source (i.e., printed) strings.

It is important to note that our procedure necessarily underestimated the time Rajan took to locate either complete or spanning strings: We required Rajan to produce the 5 digits following the target sequence to verify that he had identified the string. If Rajan has the sequence encoded as a chunk, the task may be likened to showing someone a familiar city block and requiring them to describe what is around the corner from that scene.

Method

The method for Experiments 4–6 was very similar. Thus, we give a complete description here and only note variations from the method in the next two experiments. Because these experiments involved memory search of the digits of pi, Rajan was the only subject.

Eighty 10-digit sequences were taken from the first 10,000 digits of pi. Owing to a counting error, the sequences were only approximately evenly distributed over the series with seven to nine sequences contained in each block of 1,000 digits. Forty-one of the sequences were complete strings and 39 of the sequences were spanning strings. Half the sequences came from the first 5,000 digits and half came from the second 5,000 digits. Finally, 45 of the sequences were taken from the first 30 digits in a row and 35 were taken from the last 70 digits in a row.

Each target sequence was printed in the top left corner of a 4 × 6 card. The target location and the 5-digit sequence following the target sequence were hidden from Rajan on the other side of the card. The two string types were described to him, but the two types were randomly presented. He was not told which string type he was attempting to locate during any trial.

The experimenter initiated a trial by presenting a card to Rajan when he indicated he was ready. Computer timing was initiated at that point. The trial was terminated when he called out the five-digit sequence following the target sequence. At the conclusion of each trial, the experimenter entered the target sequence location and accuracy (correct or incorrect target sequence) of the search. The computer was programmed to enter the response time and trial number into a data file.

Searches proceeded at a rate dictated by Rajan. The search task was performed in 1-hour sessions. After the first few searches, we set an upper limit of 15 minutes per search which appeared to be the upper limit of Rajan's patience.

Results

The number of searches completed per hour varied with a range of 1 to 20 searches per hour. Because many search times reached the upper limit of 15 minutes, the median search time was used as the dependent measure. To maximize the number of measures per point, we calculated the median search times separately for each string type (complete vs. spanning), row location (target sequence in first 30 vs. last 70 digits), and location in series (first 5,000 vs. last 5,000). We also tabulated the number of retrieval failures.

Retrieval Failures.   Occasionally, Rajan would announce that he was unable to find the string after 6 or 7 minutes and would not continue the search. We included those instances as retrieval failures. This memory search was very difficult for Rajan; his level of retrieval failures was 22.5%. Rajan produced twice as many retrieval failures for the spanning strings as he did for the complete strings.

String Type.   Rajan showed a clear effect of string type with a median search time of 8 seconds for complete strings and 81 seconds for spanning strings.

Location Within Row.   Rajan also showed an effect of location of the target string within the row in his search times. Rajan's median search time was 17 seconds for strings located in the first 30 digits of a row compared to 31 seconds for strings located in the last 70 digits.

Location in Series.   The location in the series also had an effect on Rajan's search time. His median search time was 18 seconds for strings located in the first 5,000 digits compared to 26 seconds for strings located in the last 5,000 digits.

Experiment 5: Five-Digit Strings

The previous experiment provided data supporting the hypothesis that Rajan has the decimal digits of pi chunked in strings of 10 as printed in the source from which he learned the digits. However, Rajan was able to locate a spanning target string of 10 digits relatively quickly because he adopted the strategy of dropping initial digits one at a time from the presented string and scanning to determine whether the remaining digits began a complete 10-digit string.

We reasoned that we could thwart Rajan's strategy by presenting 5-digit sequences which either began a complete string (starting string) or were within a complete string (internal string). We hypothesized that 5-digit starting strings would be located as quickly as 10-digit sequences corresponding to a complete string. However, 5-digit internal strings should be much more difficult to locate than 10-digit spanning strings.

Method

Eighty 5-digit sequences were taken from the first 10,000 digits of pi. Forty of the sequences corresponded to the 5 digits beginning a complete string, and 40 of the sequences were buried within a complete string. Half the sequences came from the first 5,000 digits and half came from the second 5,000 digits. Finally, half of the sequences were taken from the first 50 digits in a row and half were taken from the last 50 digits in a row.

Results

In the course of the experiment, we discovered seven duplicate 5-digit sequences. That is, we found the target sequence at a location other than the location chosen by the experimenter. In evaluating search times, the data were always sorted by the location (i.e., starting or internal string) where Rajan found the target sequence.

As in the previous experiment, we calculated the median search times separately for string type (starting vs. internal), row location (target sequence in first 50 vs. last 50 digits), and location in series (first 5,000 vs. last 5,000). As in the previous experiment, we also tabulated the number of retrieval failures.

Retrieval Failures. The task in this experiment was much more difficult for Rajan: His level of retrieval failures was 31.4% as compared to 22.5% in the previous experiment. Rajan produced three times as many retrieval failures for the internal strings as he did for the starting strings.

String Type. Rajan had a median search time of 8 seconds for starting strings compared to a median search time of 547 seconds for internal strings.

Location Within Row. As he did for the 10-digit sequences, Rajan showed a clear effect of row location. His median search time was 41 seconds for strings located in the first 50 digits of a row compared to 165 seconds for strings located in the last 50 digits.

Location in Series. Rajan also showed an effect of location in the pi series. His median search time was 52 seconds for strings located in the first 5,000 digits compared to 308 seconds for strings located in the last 5,000 digits.

Discussion

The data supported our hypothesis that, in Rajan's memory search, 5-digit starting strings would be located as quickly as 10-digit sequences corresponding to a complete string, whereas 5-digit internal strings should be much more difficult to locate than 10-digit spanning strings. Rajan had a median search time of 8 seconds for starting strings which was the same as the median search time for complete strings in the previous experiment. In contrast, his median search time was 547 seconds for internal strings compared to a median search time of 82 seconds for spanning strings in the previous experiment.

Rajan's rapid retrieval of target sequences from unspecified locations was a dramatic demonstration that chunks can exist which are unrelated to other meaningful information. When Rajan was given digits which constitute the beginning of (or an entire) 10-digit chunk, he could retrieve the following 5 digits in a median time of 8 seconds. Rajan claimed that he located the target sequence very rapidly and that much of the measured response time was spent retrieving the following 5 digits. Obviously, some of the response time must have been spent retrieving the following 5 digits, so part of Rajan's claim is certainly true.

In this task, there were 1,000 10-digit chunks that Rajan had to search to find a chunk at an unspecified location. If we ignore retrieval time for the following five digits and assume he conducted a serial search that located the target sequence, on average, halfway through the list, Rajan would have been searching at a rate of over 63 chunks per second. If we make the more reasonable assumption that retrieval of the following five digits consumed at least half the time, Rajan's estimated search rate becomes 125 chunks per second.

That search rate seems unreasonably fast to us, and we think it more likely that these chunks are accessible to Rajan in much the same way that a familiar scene is accessible to us. If we are cued for recall of a familiar scene, we probably sort through a relevant set of familiar scenes. Those scenes are categorized by their location and other relevant features (e.g., business vs. residential). Similarly, Rajan told us that he retrieved all relevant chunks beginning with a particular sequence (e.g., 623) and then checked those to ascertain which chunk continued with the target sequence. His description seems the most likely procedure to produce his very rapid response rates. It also accounts for the finding that he was equally fast at finding the chunk with both 5-digit and 10-digit cues.

Experiment 6: Starting Strings Only

Rajan located 10-digit chunks very rapidly when he was given a cue sequence in which the first digit was the beginning digit of the chunk. It did not matter whether the length of the cue sequence was 5 or 10 digits. Rajan either had direct access to the chunks (or a subset of chunks) or he scanned the chunks at a rate which, at a very conservative estimate, was over 60 chunks per second.

These two alternative hypotheses can be evaluated by considering response times. If he were scanning the chunks to locate the target sequence, response time should vary systematically with location in the row and location in the entire series.

In evaluating the scanning hypothesis, it is also important to attempt to eliminate any effects of degree of learning; chunks appearing later in the pi sequence might take longer to retrieve because they are not as well learned as chunks earlier in the sequence. This confound of degree of learning and location in the series is difficult to eliminate with certainty. However, the experiment which required Rajan to recite the rows of pi showed that the first 5,000 digits were recited with almost equal facility, but recitation time increased substantially over the last 5,000 digits. These data suggest that each of the first 5,000 digits are equally well learned. Thus, as our best approximation to evaluating the possibility that Rajan was engaging in a very rapid scan to find target sequences, we gave him a search task in which all target sequences were located in the first 5,000 digits of pi.

Method

One thousand 5-digit sequences were taken from the first 5,000 digits of pi. The 1,000 sequences consisted of two complete sets of all 5-digit sequences beginning each string of 10 digits in the series.

The sequences were presented by computer. In all other respects, the procedure was identical to that used in the previous experiment.

Results

We calculated the median search time distribution as well as the median search times for location in the 5,000-digit series and location within a row. The latter condition was included because Rajan showed a strong within-row location effect in the studies in which he had to search for specific locations. We also calculated Rajan's error rate.

Error Rate.   Rajan's error rate was 9.3%, which demonstrates that this was a very difficult task for him. His error rate did not vary systematically with location in the series or location in a row.

Search Time Distribution.   The distribution of search times was markedly skewed. All search times of 30 seconds and faster are presented in Fig. 5.5. There were 136 search times slower than 30 seconds, and the median search time was 4.0 seconds.

Location in Series.   The search times were sorted by 5-row block to determine whether search time was dependent on the location of the target sequence in the 5,000-digit series. The median search time for each 5-row block is shown in Table 5.2. Inspection of these data confirm that search times did not vary in a systematic way with the location of the target in the series.

Location in Row.   The search times were sorted by each 10-digit string within each row to determine whether search time was dependent on the location of the target sequence in a row. The median search time for each 10-digit row

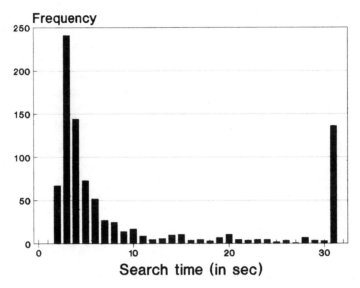

FIG. 5.5.   Distribution of correct search times given a 5-digit sequence beginning a printed string.

block is also shown in Table 5.2. These data confirm that search times also did
not vary systematically with the location of the search target in a row.

The median search time of 4.0 seconds, taken together with the data showing
that search times did not vary systematically with location in the series or row,
strongly suggests that Rajan's description of his search process was correct. That
is, he immediately retrieved all relevant chunks beginning with a particular se-

TABLE 5.2
Median Response Time to Locate a Sequence in the 5,000-Digit Series or
Within a Row in Seconds. The Series Data Are Grouped by Five-Row Block and the
Row Data Are Grouped by 10-Digit String

	Median Response Time	
Block #	5,000-Digit Series	Within-Row
1	4.0	3.0
2	4.4	5.1
3	3.4	3.4
4	5.2	4.1
5	3.6	3.4
6	3.3	4.4
7	3.2	4.0
8	3.8	4.3
9	4.3	4.7
10	4.8	4.6

quence and determined which was the target sequence; then he recited the rest of the target chunk.

His median retrieval time was half that in previous experiments in which the search was over 10,000 rather than 5,000 digits. Given that these data suggest there was no systematic location effect in the first 5,000 digits of pi, we propose that the difference in search time can be attributed to the familiarity of the chunks. Once he has learned the digits on a page (5,000 digits), Rajan tends to rehearse those digits in page blocks. Because he has had numerous interviews or demonstrations during which he recites portions of the first pages, the first 5,000 digits have been rehearsed much more than the second 5,000 digits of pi. This differential familiarity was demonstrated clearly in Experiment 2 in which the time to recite a row was fairly constant on the first page (i.e., first 5,000 digits) but increased dramatically over the second 5,000 digits.

GENERAL DISCUSSION

These experiments enable us to describe with considerable confidence Rajan's procedure for retrieving digits from designated locations in the first 10,000 digits of pi. We can also delineate the manner in which he has these digits stored in memory. We conclude that Rajan has the digits stored in chunks of 10 digits which are further grouped into rows of 10 chunks. The rows play a central role in Rajan's strategy for retrieving digits from designated locations. The 10-digit chunks allow Rajan to accurately retrieve digit sequences from unspecified locations in the first 10,000 digits of pi.

Retrieving Digits of pi at Specified Locations

We conclude that Rajan makes very effective use of location information (Experiments 1, 2, and 3). He retrieves digits at specific locations of pi by retrieving the appropriate row very quickly (taking approximately 1.5 seconds) and then counting over to the specified location. Finding the location within a row takes over five times as long as locating the row.

The speed with which Rajan locates a row makes it obvious that the first column is substantially overlearned relative to most rows. To make that point, consider retrieval, with the row given, from the first 2,500 digits of pi. We know that Rajan rehearses previous digits of pi as he learns additional blocks; thus, the earliest digits of pi should show considerable overlearning relative to later digits. Nevertheless, the median search time for a target digit at locations 10–29 within each row in the first 2,500 digits of pi was 3.6 seconds. It took him twice as long to locate a digit in the first 30 digits of a very well-learned row as it did to locate *any* row in the first 10,000 digits of pi. Note that, because the searches were restricted to the first 10,000 digits of pi, the number of rows in that set is the same as the number of digits within a row (100).

It should be clear from our description that Rajan has the digits of pi organized as a large matrix with rows of length 100. Rajan told us that his procedure for learning any large matrix of numbers is to learn each row and then keep track of the rows by using the first column as a marker. He uses serial position as a location marker for digits within a row and rows within the series of 10,000 digits. His procedure allows him to retrieve any row very rapidly by using the first column.

We substantiated his report with an experiment in chapter 3 in which Rajan was required to recite randomly selected rows and columns from 6 × 6 and 12 × 12 matrices. In that experiment, Rajan recalled the first column approximately at the same rate as any of the rows. By contrast, the other columns took much longer to recall than the rows. Those data were from newly learned matrices, while the present searches (of pi) were performed with a matrix for which Rajan has had extensive practice.

Retrieving Sequences of pi from Unspecified Locations

We have also shown in Experiments 4, 5, and 6 that Rajan can rapidly retrieve target sequences from unspecified locations. These data are a dramatic demonstration that effective chunks, which are unrelated to other information, can exist. When Rajan was given digits that constitute the beginning of (or an entire) 10-digit chunk from the first 10,000 digits of pi, he could retrieve the following 5 digits in a median time of 8 seconds. When the set was reduced to 5,000 digits, median retrieval time was reduced to 4 seconds.

Because median retrieval time was directly related to the size of the search set, it is tempting to conclude that the retrieval time reflected the time needed to rapidly scan the search set. However, the data from the 5,000-digit search set show that is not the case because retrieval time did not vary with location in the 5,000-digit set. Rajan claimed that his procedure was to retrieve all relevant chunks beginning with a particular sequence (e.g., 623) and then check those to ascertain which chunk continued with the target sequence.

Rajan chunked the decimal digits of pi in 10-digit chunks only because that is the way the digits appear in the source material. The chunks are unrelated to any other material; however, they are effective for Rajan in that they can be rapidly searched by category (e.g., those chunks that begin with 623). He provides a dramatic demonstration that effective chunking can occur without reference to other meaningful material.

The present set of experiments demonstrates how Rajan has the digits of pi organized in memory and that those digits are chunked in 10-digit strings. It is also clear that he has very rapid access to a 10-digit chunk. The obvious next step is to determine the nature of that access. We report on those experiments in chapter 7.

CHAPTER 6

Searching for Locations
in a Visual Display

The data from Rajan's memory search of the first 10,000 decimal digits of pi demonstrated that his organization of those digits in memory corresponded exactly to the way the digits were printed in Shanks and Wrench (1962). We wondered whether Rajan would use his fairly efficient memory search procedure in a comparable visual search task.

Visual search tasks usually employ large sets of items randomly arranged with the subject required to locate a specific item (Neisser, 1964, pp. 66–71). However, the experiments reported here involve search for locations rather than items. This difference was intentional because we wanted to compare these results with those of the previous chapter.

We speculated that if Rajan used his memory search procedure to locate digits on the printed sheets of pi, his visual search might differ from the visual search used by control subjects. Specifically, we thought the control subjects might have to count down the rows to get to the correct row, whereas Rajan might be able to get there immediately. Then, both Rajan and the control subjects would have to count over to get to the correct digit. Stated differently, we thought Rajan would be faster than the control subjects in a visual search, and the difference would all be attributable to the time taken to locate the appropriate row.

SEARCHING FOR LOCATIONS IN A VISUAL DISPLAY

Three of the control subjects (DA, GN, and MD) participated in this experiment. The fourth control subject (TH) was not available during the summer this experiment was conducted. The physical layout for each page of the source material is shown in Fig. 5.1. Four pages (20,000 digits) were used for this experiment. The four pages were arranged on a 18 × 24 in (46 × 61 cm) corkboard with the first 5,000 digits in the upper left-hand quadrant, the next 5,000 digits directly below, the third set of 5,000 digits in the upper right-hand quadrant, and the final set of 5,000 digits in the lower right-hand quadrant.

Method

A computer program was created to sample 4,000 digit locations from the 20,000 digits. The 20,000 locations were blocked in groups of five (i.e., each printed block of 10 was divided in half) and a location was randomly sampled from each 5-digit block. Those 4,000 locations were then randomized for presentation in the search task.

The search procedure was identical to that used in the memory search experiments. The subjects were seated facing a computer monitor with the corkboard in their lap. The experimenter both initiated and terminated a trial by pressing the spacebar. Experimenter control was used so that the subjects would not terminate the trial in anticipation of locating the target digit. When the subjects indicated they were ready, the trial number and the target location (e.g., 4,782) were presented in the center of the screen. The trial was terminated when the subject called out the target digit. The experimenter had a printout containing the trial number, target digit location, and target digit to verify the accuracy of the search. The trial number, target location, response time, and accuracy (correct or incorrect target digit) of the search were recorded.

Search trials proceeded at a rate dictated by the subject. The search task was performed in 1 hour sessions. Subjects varied greatly in the number of searches completed per hour with a range of 73 to 550 searches per hour. On one occasion, Rajan did 550 searches in 1 hour with one error.

Results

Error Rate. All subjects were reasonably accurate in this search task with mean error rates ranging from 1.0% to 2.6%. They showed a slight improvement over trials with a mean error rate of 2.8% during the first 500 trials and a mean error rate of 1.4% on the last 500 trials. Rajan had the lowest overall error rate (1.0%) and the highest initial error rate (3.4%).

Search Times. We treated these data in the same way as we treated Rajan's memory search data. Because the data are skewed, we took the median search time as most representative. Response times under .2 second were excluded from the calculation of the median because they obviously represented experimenter error.

Rajan's median visual search time for digits at specific locations was much faster (4.4 seconds) than his comparable median memory search time (13.0 seconds). The median search times for GN, DA, and MD were 3.8, 5.4, and 7.3 seconds, respectively.

Search Process. We calculated the median search time for consecutive blocks of 1,000 digits. Those data are shown separately for each subject in Figs. 6.1 through 6.4.

Inspection of these data made it quite clear that subjects began their search by locating the appropriate page and then searched for the correct 1,000 block within that page. These data clearly show that subjects *did not* perform a serial search for the correct row in the 20,000 digits. Thus, we constructed a model of visual search suggested by the data.

A PROCESS MODEL FOR LOCATING DIGITS IN A VISUAL DISPLAY

These data suggest that subjects began by locating the correct page and then searching for the correct 1,000 block within that page. After they found the correct 1,000 block, we assumed that subjects proceeded to find the appropriate row (100 block), the appropriate block of 10 within the row, and, finally, the appropriate digit within the block of 10. If our assumptions were correct, we should see systematic search patterns for pages, 1,000 blocks within pages, rows (of 100) within 1,000 blocks, blocks of 10 within rows, and digits within 10 blocks.

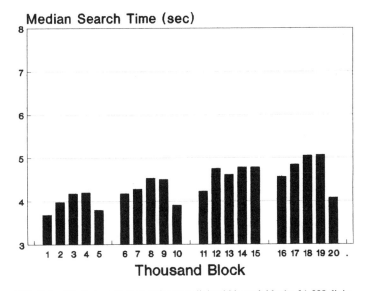

FIG. 6.1. Median search time to locate a digit within each block of 1,000 digits. These data are from Rajan.

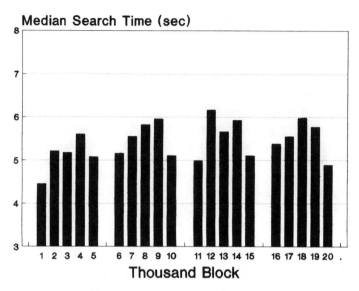

FIG. 6.2. Median search time to locate a digit within each block of 1,000 digits. These data are from subject DA.

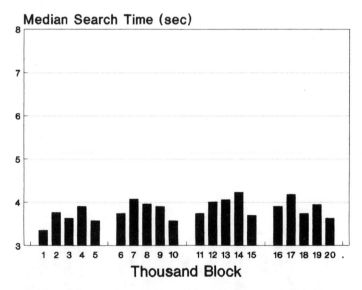

FIG. 6.3. Median search time to locate a digit within each block of 1,000 digits. These data are from subject GN.

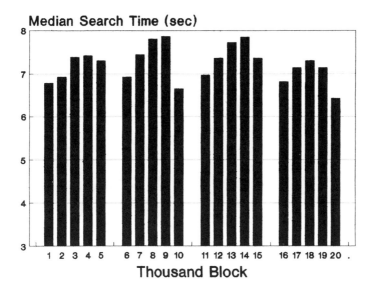

FIG. 6.4. Median search time to locate a digit within each block of 1,000 digits. These data are from subject MD.

Accordingly, we sorted the data separately for each of those categories (i.e., pages, 1,000 blocks, etc.). The results of those sorts are shown in Figs. 6.5 through 6.9. Using rows (100 blocks) as an example, all subjects showed a systematic variation in search times with exterior rows (i.e., first and last rows) found more rapidly than the corresponding interior locations. The same result was obtained for 1,000 blocks within pages, 10 blocks within a row, and digits within a 10 block.

The only deviation from the general pattern showing an advantage for exterior blocks was in Rajan's data for pages. He showed steadily increasing median search times over pages. The control subjects showed the typical advantage for the last page.

Deriving the Components of the Model

Given the systematic variation in search times demonstrated previously, we hypothesized that the total search time could be broken down into an encoding/production time plus the time to find each of the component locations (page, 1,000 block within page, 100 block within 1,000 block, 10 block within row, and digit within 10 block). We assumed that the search proceeded in the order just stated (i.e., page, 1,000 block, etc.). Finally, we assumed that the encoding/production time included the time to read and interpret the location to be found as well as the time to read and produce the digit at the target location.

The structure of the data allowed us to evaluate the average time taken for

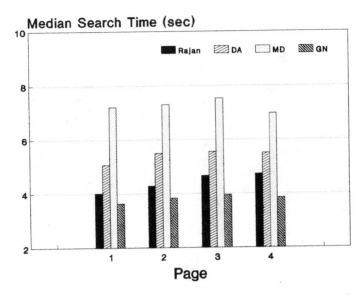

FIG. 6.5. Median search time to locate a page. The data are presented separately for each subject.

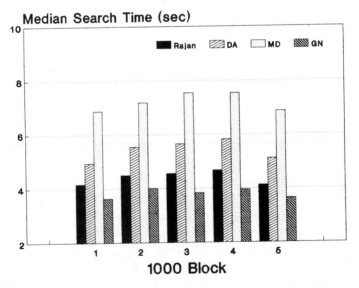

FIG. 6.6. Median search time to locate a 1,000-block within a page. The data are presented separately for each subject.

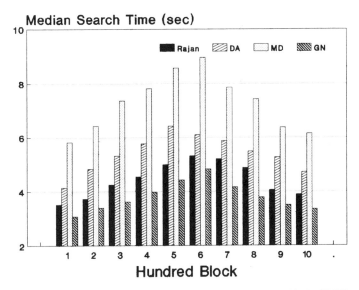

FIG. 6.7.   Median search time to locate a row (100 block) within a block of 1,000 digits. The data are presented separately for each subject.

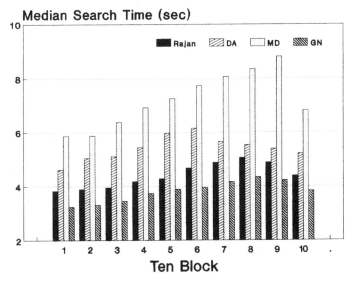

FIG. 6.8.   Median search time to locate a 10 block within a row (100 block). The data are presented separately for each subject.

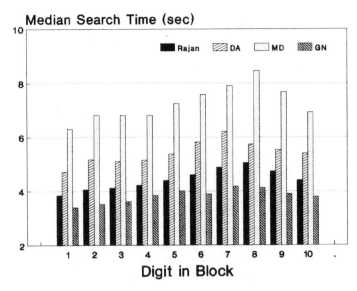

FIG. 6.9. Median search time to locate a digit within a block of 10 digits. The
data are presented separately for each subject.

each step of our proposed search process. Note that when we calculated the median search time for levels of a component location (e.g., rows within 1,000
blocks), every level of every other component location (e.g., page, 1,000-blocks,
etc.) was represented equally often at each level of the target component (e.g.,
row 1, row 2, etc.). Thus, the differences in search times among the levels of
a component are not contaminated by other search components—they represent
true differences.

The shortest search time for a target component includes the search times for
all other components (e.g., page, 1,000-blocks, etc.) as well as the time to get
from the preceding component to the target component. The time to get from
the preceding component is the key to determining the average search time for
a target component (e.g., rows). That time cannot be derived from the data. In
order to compute average search times, we made the assumption that a minimum
median time of .1 second was necessary to get from one component to the next.

Take rows as an example. We assume subjects find the correct page, then the
correct 1,000 block, and then the correct row within that 1,000 block. If we assume that it took .1 second to get to the row with the shortest search time after
finding the correct 1,000 block, then the time to get to the other rows after locating the correct 1,000 block can be easily computed.

The computational procedure is illustrated using the 100 block (i.e., row within 1,000 block) data for subject MD. That data is presented in Table 6.1. As
noted earlier, we take the location with the fastest median search time (in these
data, row 1) and assume that it took a median time of .1 second to locate that

TABLE 6.1
Median Search Times for Each Row (100 Block Within 1,000 Blocks) for Subject
MD. Also Presented Are the Hypothetical Times to Locate Each Row after
Locating the Correct 1,000 Block

Row	Median Search Time	Location Time
1	5.8	.1*
2	6.4	.7
3	7.4	1.7
4	7.8	2.1
5	8.6	2.9
6	9.0	3.3
7	7.9	2.2
8	7.4	1.7
9	6.4	.7
10	6.1	.4

*Hypothetical time for fastest search.

row after locating the 1,000 block in which the row is located. Given that assumption, it follows that the time to locate any target row after locating the correct 1,000 block is the difference between the baseline time (the median search time for the fastest row minus .1 second) and the median search time for the target row. To illustrate, if it took a median time of .1 second to locate row 1 (which has a median search time of 5.8 seconds), then it must have taken a median time of .7 seconds to locate row 2 (6.4 seconds minus 5.7 seconds). The median time for subject MD to locate each target row is also given in Table 6.1.

Using this procedure, we calculated the median time to locate each page, 1,000 block within page, 100 block (row) within 1,000 block, 10 block within row, and digit within 10 block separately for each subject. We then calculated the average time to locate each component (i.e., page, 1,000 block, etc.) by taking the mean of the median location times for each level of the component. Using the data in Table 6.1 as an example, the mean of the median times for subject MD to locate rows was 1.58 seconds.

Finally, the hypothetical encoding/production time was derived by subtracting each component mean search time from the overall median response time. The results of those computations are shown, separately for each subject, in Fig. 6.10. As can be seen, the pattern of results was the same for all subjects. For all subjects, including Rajan, the longest time component was the encoding/production time. That is not surprising because the encoding/production component includes at least two logically separable processes: the time to read and interpret the location to be found (encoding) and the time to read and produce the digit at the target location (production).

Subjects found the correct page and 1,000 block within that page rather quickly but took more time to find the correct row (100 block), 10 block within row, and correct digit within the 10 block. That theoretical pattern of responses not

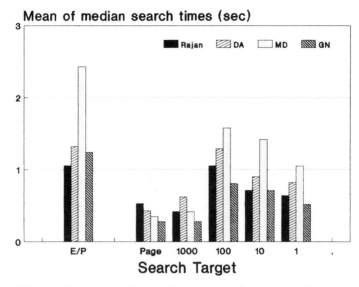

FIG. 6.10.   Theoretical median encoding/production time together with the mean of the median search times to locate a page, 1,000 block, 100 block, 10-digit block, or single digit within a 10-digit block. The data are presented separately for each subject.

only fits the data presented here, but it is also consistent with our observations during the search sessions and the subjects' subjective observations. Subjects particularly remarked on the difficulty of finding the correct row during the visual search.

APPLYING THE MODEL TO RAJAN'S MEMORY SEARCH

In the previous chapter, we presented data supporting Rajan's claim that, in a memory search, he went directly to the correct row and then searched the row for the target location. If his claim were correct, then the process model for locating digits in a visual display should not work when applied to Rajan's memory search. To demonstrate that point, we sorted Rajan's memory search data and derived hypothetical median response times for each component using the procedure described previously. The results are presented in Fig. 6.11. Those calculations demonstrate that our theoretical visual search process cannot be applied to Rajan's memory search. Obviously, Rajan could not have a negative encoding/production time!

The negative encoding/production time is not the result of our assumption that it takes a minimum of .1 second to move from one component to another. If we were to make the extremely conservative (and logically untenable) assumption

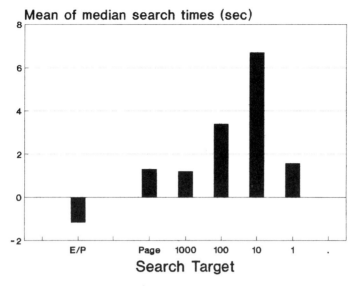

FIG. 6.11. Theoretical median encoding/production time together with the mean of the median search times to locate a page, 1,000 block, 100 block, 10-digit block, or single digit within a 10-digit block. These are the memory search data from Rajan.

that it took no time to move between components, the visual search model would still produce a negative encoding/production time for Rajan's memory search data.

Modeling Rajan's Memory Search

The data from Rajan's memory search (described in the previous chapter) suggest that he quickly found the correct row and then searched the row to find the correct digit. Because the data also show that Rajan has the digits chunked in groups of 10, we assumed that Rajan's memory search would consist of first locating the target row, then locating the correct 10-block within the row, and finally locating the target digit within the 10-block. A direct estimate of Rajan's time to locate a row was provided in Experiment 2 of the preceding chapter. We used those data (presented in Table 5.1) to derive the theoretical row location component for Rajan's memory search. As before, we assumed that it took .1 second to locate the row(s) with the fastest median search time. We then used the same procedure described earlier for the visual search components to estimate the mean (of the median) location time for rows. The other components (i.e., 10-block, target digit within 10-block, and encoding/ production time) were estimated exactly as described earlier for the visual search components.

The results of these computations for Rajan's memory search are presented in Fig. 6.12. The pattern of the hypothetical components matches our empirical

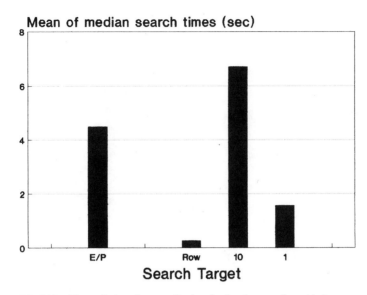

FIG. 6.12. Theoretical median encoding/production time together with the mean of the median search times to locate a row, 10-digit block, or single digit within a 10-digit block. These are the memory search data from Rajan.

observations as well as Rajan's descriptions of his memory search. More importantly, the pattern is quite different from a visual search.

In Rajan's visual search, the largest amount of time was spent as encoding/production time, with the largest search component spent locating the correct row. In contrast, the largest component in Rajan's memory search was the time spent locating the correct chunk of digits within a row. Because our data show that Rajan treated the 10-blocks as chunks, we think it makes sense that it would more difficult to assess the order of the chunks than to find a particular digit within the chunk. Put differently, examining the chunk (to locate the target digit) was a small problem relative to making sure that the correct chunk was being examined.

The theoretical components also match Rajan's claim for memory search. He stated, "I go directly to the row and then locate the target digit within the row." The row location component was the smallest of all components rather than the largest of the search components.

Finally, we note that the theoretical encoding/ production component in memory search was about three times the duration of the encoding/production component in visual search. The time to read the target location or produce the target digit should not vary; thus we are led to speculate that the encoding/production component in a memory search also must include other activities such as verification time.

CONCLUSIONS

Visual search for all subjects, including Rajan, proceeded systematically and quickly through the page, 1,000-block within page, row within 1,000-block, 10-block within row, and digit within 10-block to the correct location. With practice, the visual search became both fast and accurate. The mean error rate of 1.4% on the last 500 trials is, in our view, quite an impressive performance.

A comparison of the hypothetical median location times for Rajan's visual and memory search makes three important points: First, the visual search model works for Rajan's visual search but produces an impossible result when applied to memory search. Taken together with the data presented in the previous chapters, it is clear that Rajan's memory search was substantially different from his visual search. We should note here that Rajan began the visual search assuming that he would use his memory to facilitate the search. He abandoned that strategy after about 100 trials when he realized that his attempts to combine visual and memory search were producing a relatively high error rate.

Second, the incompatibility of Rajan's visual and memory searches for digits at specific locations of pi add support to our conclusion that Rajan does not use visual imagery in his memory search. It seems to us that the evidence for that conclusion is overwhelming.

Finally, a modification of the visual search model in an attempt to capture Rajan's memory search produced components which are consistent with the data from, and observations of, his memory search.

Priming Digit Strings

The two purposes of the research described in this chapter are to evaluate the priming of, and retrieval cues for, chunks in the first 10,000 decimal digits of pi. As we did in the memory search experiments, we concentrated on the first 10,000 decimal digits of pi because those digits have been extremely well learned by Rajan with the first 5,000 digits particularly well rehearsed.

The memory search studies with Rajan described in chapter 5 demonstrated that he has the digits of pi chunked in 10-digit blocks in memory. We assume he chunked the digits that way because that is the way the digits appear in the source material. The chunks appear to be unrelated to any other material; Rajan reported they are effective in that they can be rapidly searched by category (e.g., those chunks that begin with 623). The memory search studies in chapter 5 provide a convincing demonstration that chunking can occur without reference to other meaningful material.

Those studies also demonstrated that he has very rapid access to a 10-digit chunk. One obvious next step was to determine the nature of that access. We assumed that the 10-digit chunks constitute a subset of Rajan's lexicon. Much research has been done on the nature of lexical access with the major theoretical models either assuming a search process (e.g., Rubenstein, Garfield, & Millikan, 1970; Rubenstein, Lewis, & Rubenstein, 1971) or direct access to the lexicon (Morton, 1969, 1970). As a first approximation, we believe that Morton's logogen model (1969, 1970) is appropriate to describe Rajan's access to the 10-digit chunks. Briefly put, Morton (1970) defines a logogen "in terms of the usual understanding of 'word' " (p. 206). He argues that a logogen is activated by visual, verbal, and contextual information. Our earlier studies, together with informal tests, strongly suggest that Rajan essentially has immediate access to a digit string with either visual or verbal presentation. The interesting problem remaining is to determine what sort of information (if any) might serve as a context to prime access to a digit string.

Rajan's comments and performance suggest two possibilities: First, he stated that, when given a target sequence, he retrieves all relevant chunks beginning with the first few digits (e.g., 623) to check for the correct sequence. This suggests that retrieval of a target sequence such as 62371 would be primed (i.e., speed of access would be increased) by a sequence of the form 623xy (where x and y are digits picked randomly with the restriction that they not duplicate any digits in the target sequence). Priming should occur whether the 623xy sequence is a legitimate target sequence or a foil sequence.

Second, Rajan often specified the 1,000-block location when he retrieved the 5 digits following a 5-digit target string. Recall that his errors in retrieving specific digits of pi were often location errors in which he retrieved 10-digit strings adjacent to the target block. Taken together, the location information and error data suggest that retrieval of a target sequence might prime retrieval of adjacent targets.

In short, similarity (of sequence) and location information may act as context for Rajan when he is retrieving digit sequences from pi. Before testing for context effects, we demonstrated that priming can occur for Rajan under our testing procedure. For that demonstration, we repeated target and foil sequences with the assumption that priming should occur if the lag between repetitions was not too large. As the final set of experiments in this series, we established which elements in the 10-digit block carry the most information by using a procedure in which sequences with missing elements were presented. For Rajan, this task is the numerical equivalent of a word fragment completion task where subjects are given a word with missing elements (e.g., __ar__va__ __ for "aardvark") and asked to complete the word.

Experiment 1: Repetition Priming

We begin this report with a procedure designed to demonstrate that priming can occur for numerical sequences. Our test procedure is comparable to a lexical decision task with the target strings being number sequences rather than words. In a lexical decision task, the subject has to decide whether the presented string of letters is a word or is not a word. Rajan had to decide whether the presented string of digits was or was not taken from the beginning of a 10-digit block.

The targets in this study were 5-digit sequences, which began a 10-digit block in the first 5,000 digits of pi. As we noted above, our research strongly suggests that Rajan treats those 10-digit blocks as chunks. The foils differed from the targets in two respects: (a) they were taken from the second 5,000 digits of pi, and (b) the sequence began near the middle of a 10-digit block.

Our earlier experiments with Rajan demonstrated that he has complete mastery of the first 10,000 digits of pi. In addition, those data clearly reflect much more practice on the first 5,000 digits than the second 5,000. That is why we used the sequences from the first 5,000 digits as targets and constructed the foils with sequences taken from the second 5,000 digits.

It is important to note that we present the experiments in this chapter in the order we think tells the clearest story. The repetition priming procedure presented here was the last priming procedure Rajan was given. Thus, he was very practiced and showed nearly peak performance in speed and accuracy in these data.

Method

As in all our experiments, the materials on which Rajan was tested were taken from the source he used to memorize the decimal digits of pi (Shanks & Wrench, 1962). Figure 5.1 reproduces a page (5,000 digits) from that source. A computer program was created to randomly select target and foil sequences from the first 10,000 digits of pi. The target sequences were selected from the first 5,000 digits, and the foil sequences were selected from the second 5,000 digits. Sampling was random and without replacement. The first and last string of 10 digits in any row, and the first and last rows (of 100 digits) from each 5,000-digit block were not included. This process was repeated when all elements (i.e., all 10-digit blocks) had been sampled. Targets were the first 5 digits in a 10-digit string, and foils were digits 4 through 8 in a 10-digit string.

Rajan responded to target and foil sequences repeated with lags of 0, 2, 4, 6, or 8 intervening sequences in addition to target and foil sequences which were not repeated. Type of sequence (target or foil), repetition of sequence (repeated or not), and lag for repeated sequence (0, 2, 4, 6, or 8) were randomly generated by a computer program with the restriction that a series containing a repeated sequence be completed before another repeated sequence could be generated. Rajan completed 10,000 trials on this task which produced approximately 4,000 errorless trials each for nonrepeated target and foil sequences as well as approximately 140 errorless trials for each lag for both repeated target and foil sequences.

For this experiment, Rajan read the sequences from a computer monitor. He both initiated and terminated each trial by pressing the spacebar. When Rajan initiated a trial, the word "READY" was presented in the center of the screen. Shortly (.75 second) after the READY signal, the digit string was presented in the same location. Rajan responded by pressing "q" with his left (preferred) hand if the sequence was a target and "p" with his right hand if the sequence was a foil. Feedback on errors was provided by a computer beep. Following each trial, the computer recorded the trial number, sequence location, type of trial, reaction time, and response accuracy (correct or not correct). Trials continued at a rate dictated by Rajan. The task rarely continued for more than 1 hour. Rajan paced himself with breaks when he felt they were necessary. He was instructed to take a break whenever he thought the error rate was increasing.

A Statistical Note

The reader will undoubtedly have noted that, up to this point, we have not used statistics in describing our data. That has been a deliberate choice based on our view that the data were either descriptive or the critical differences were obvious. These priming data are quite different. The differences between conditions are small, and it is important to determine whether they are reliable. Therefore, we performed statistical analyses on these data.

Because the distribution for the priming data is markedly skewed, we have used trimmed data in these analyses; hence, the means reported are trimmed means. The advantage of using trimmed means has been discussed in detail by many authors (e.g., Wilcox, 1992). Our procedure for trimming the data was to eliminate all scores lying outside boundaries which were defined by three times the interquartile range added to the upper and lower bounds of that range. The interquartile range (also called the *fourth spread* or *F-spread*) is the range spanned in an ordered array by the middle 50% of the scores. The data were trimmed separately for every condition (e.g., unprimed target, unprimed foil, lag two target, lag two foil, etc.). Over all the experiments reported in this chapter, the trimming procedure eliminated between 1.1% and 13.2% of the data from individual conditions. The range and median percentage of the data trimmed will be given for each experiment.

Results

We tabulated Rajan's overall error rate for target and foil baseline (i.e., nonrepeated sequence) conditions as well as for each lag condition, error rate by 2,500-trial block, and the mean search time for correct searches in each condition. Those data are presented separately.

Error Rate.   Rajan showed a reduction in overall error rate over the 10,000 trials. His overall error rate for each successive 2,500 trial block was 8.1, 5.0, 3.8, and 4.1%, respectively. His overall error rate for the targets was 4.7%, and his overall error rate for foils was 5.2%.

Rajan's error rate was higher for nonrepeated sequences than for repeated sequences but did not vary systematically with lag. The error rate for each lag and for nonrepeated sequences is shown in Table 7.1.

Repetition reduced the error rate for both targets and foils. Furthermore, both the absolute and relative reduction in error rate was greater for targets than for foils. Repetition reduced the absolute error rate 2.6% for targets and 1.7% for foils. That translated into a relative reduction in error rate of 57% and 26% for targets and foils, respectively.

Mean Search Time.   Trimmed distributions were used to compute the mean search times. The amount of data trimmed in each condition ranged from 1.1% to 13.2%. The median percentage trim was 7.9%. The mean search times for

TABLE 7.1
Percent Error for Each Lag and for Nonrepeated
Items Presented Separately for Targets and Foils

Condition	Target	Foil
Nonrepeated	4.7	6.4
Lag 0	1.2	5.4
Lag 2	1.5	3.9
Lag 4	3.2	5.1
Lag 6	1.3	6.7
Lag 8	3.1	2.4

the baseline (i.e., nonrepeated) condition and each lag condition are presented in Fig. 7.1. As can be seen, targets were identified more rapidly than foils, $F(1, 9224) = 226.25$, MSE $= 1.74$, $p < .001$. The nonrepeated sequences took longer to identify than the repeated sequences, $F(6, 9224) = 58.06$, MSE $= 1.74$, $p < .001$. An immediate repetition reduced the time to make a decision by at least 50% relative to a nonrepeated sequence, and that was true for both targets and foils. Subsequent analyses confirmed the visual impression from Fig. 7.1. That is, as lag increased, the time to make the decision increased fairly systematically for both targets and foils.

In short, the data show strong repetition priming. As would be anticipated, the magnitude of the effect was systematically reduced as the interval between

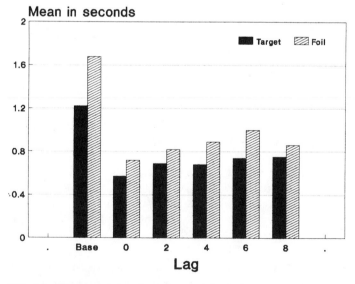

FIG. 7.1. Mean search time for the target and foil baseline conditions as well as for each lag condition.

the two repetitions was increased. The only unexpected effect was that repetition produced a greater reduction in error rate for targets than for foils.

Experiments 2–4: Similarity and Location Primes (First 5,000 Digits)

The first experiment demonstrated that repetition priming can occur in this numerical approximation of the lexical decision task. The next question is whether Rajan can be primed with the equivalent of context cues. As we stated at the beginning of this chapter, Rajan's comments and performance suggest that the most likely candidates for context cues are similarity and location primes. Thus, similarity and location relationships were used in the next series of tests for potential priming effects.

Each priming test consisted of 2,400 trials, which we have elected to designate as an experiment. Because Rajan began with a fairly high error rate, we ran six 2,400-trial experiments in an attempt to reduce that error rate. We alternated the target sequences in the experiments between the first and second 5,000 digits of pi in order to keep practice effects on the task roughly comparable for both sets of digits. For convenience, we designated the three experiments on the first 5,000 digits as Experiments 2–4 and the three experiments on the second 5,000 digits as Experiments 5–7. Rajan always knew which 5,000 digits were being tested in these experiments.

We conducted separate tests of priming on the two sets of digits because Rajan showed a substantial difference in performance on the two sets of digits in other tests. As will be seen, performance when targets were taken from the second 5,000 digits was not as good as when the targets were from the first 5,000 digits. That outcome occurred even though Rajan always had the benefit of an additional 2,400 trials of practice on the task when the targets were from the second set of digits. Here we report the three experiments using the first 5,000 digits of pi as targets.

Method

There were four types of similarity relationships and four types of location relationships which served as potential primes. In each experiment, there were 1,200 targets and 1,200 foils. There were 100 targets for each of the eight types of relationships and 400 targets that were not primed (but served as potential location primes). The foils consisted of 400 similarity relationships (100 for each type of similarity) and 800 foils generated as in Experiment 1.

Similarity Relationships. Rajan claimed that a target sequence such as 62371 would be primed by a sequence of the form 623xy (where x and y are digits picked randomly with the restriction that they not duplicate any digits in the target sequence). Although Rajan identified the first three digits as the important cue, we wondered whether other digit sequences having digits in common with the target sequence might be effective as primes. Therefore, we used the similarity relationship Rajan specified, along with three others, as potential primes.

Given the target sequence 62371, the four types of similarity relationships were: (S1) 623*xy*; (S2) *x*237*y*; (S3) *xy*371; and (S4) 6*x*3*y*1. All potential similarity primes were necessarily foils; that is, they were not sequences starting a 10-digit block in the first 5,000 digits.

Location Relationships. In the case of the location relationships, both the target and the potential prime were targets. That is, both started a 10-digit block in the first 5,000 digits of pi. We attempted to prime critical targets by other starting sequences physically surrounding them on the source sheets. The four types of location relationships were described by the location of the 10-digit sequence from which the potential prime was taken. They were as follows: the sequence immediately preceded the target block (L1); the sequence was in the same location as the target block but was in the preceding row (i.e., it was immediately *above* the target block−L2); the sequence was in the same location as the target block but was in the following row (i.e., it was immediately *below* the target block−L3); and the sequence immediately followed the target block (L4).

Except for the type of potential prime, the procedure was identical to that used in the first experiment.

Results

We tabulated Rajan's error rate for each condition and the mean search time for correct searches in each condition. We also tabulated the same data separately for foils generated as similarity primes and foils taken from the second 5,000 digits. There were no systematic differences in either errors or search time between the two types of foils generated in these experiments so we pooled the foil data.

We did two analyses on each experiment. The first analysis compared unprimed targets and foils. The second analysis compared unprimed targets with targets in the eight priming conditions. All data are presented separately for each experiment.

Error Rate. The error rate data are shown separately for each experiment in Table 7.2. These data show that the error rate for both primed and unprimed targets was quite high in Experiment 2 but showed a systematic reduction over the next two experiments. By contrast, there was no systematic reduction in error rate for foils over the three experiments.

A finer grain examination shows that the error rate for primed targets was

TABLE 7.2
Percent Errors for Unprimed Targets, Foils, and
Primed Targets in Each Similarity and Location Condition.
The Targets Are from the First 5,000 Digits of pi

Condition	Experiment 2	Experiment 3	Experiment 4
Foil	7.1	11.5	7.8
Unprimed Target	9.5	7.2	7.7
S1	13.0	5.0	8.0
S2	17.0	9.0	4.0
S3	10.0	6.0	6.0
S4	14.0	5.0	5.1
L1	9.0	7.0	5.0
L2	15.0	20.0	8.0
L3	22.0	14.0	7.0
L4	11.0	13.1	10.0

higher than all but one of the error rates for unprimed targets in the first experiment. The higher error rate for primed targets persisted in the second experiment in three of the four conditions where the location of the prime was manipulated. With additional practice (i.e., in Experiment 3), the higher error rate for primed targets was eliminated entirely.

Mean Search Time. The mean search times for the target and foil baseline conditions as well as each similarity and location priming condition are presented separately for each experiment in Figs. 7.2, 7.3, and 7.4. Trimmed means were used to compute the mean search times. The amount of data trimmed in each condition ranged from 1.4 to 11.6%. The median percentage trim was 6.3%. As can be seen, there was a marked difference between the target and foil in all three experiments, $F_2(1, 1413) = 164.68$, MSE $= 2.10$, p $< .01$; $F_3(1, 1351) = 73.24$, MSE $= .59$, p $< .01$; $F_4(1, 1426) = 56.24$, MSE $= 1.52$, p $< .01$.

There was no priming effect the first time Rajan attempted this task. When priming occurs, response time is reduced for primed targets. A subsequent Newman–Keuls test showed that the S4 similarity prime produced reliably longer response times than all other conditions. However, after Rajan gained some experience on the task, the S1 similarity prime (in which the first three digits of the prime are the same as the first three digits of the primed target) produced shorter response times, $F_3(8, 1003) = 5.05$, MSE $= .15$, $p < .01$; $F_4(8, 1043) = 6.00$, MSE $= .36$, $p < .01$. In the last experiment on the first 5,000 digits, the S2 similarity prime also produced a reliably faster response time than that for the unprimed targets. No other priming condition had a reliable effect.

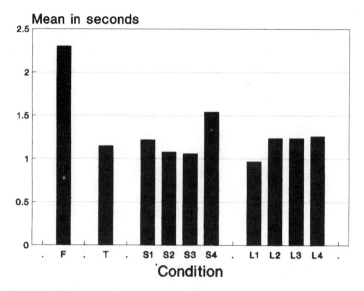

FIG. 7.2. Mean search times for the target and foil baseline conditions as well as for each similarity and location-priming condition. These data are from Experiment 2.

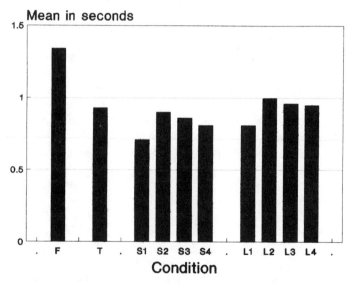

FIG. 7.3. Mean search times for the target and foil baseline conditions as well as for each similarity and location-priming condition. These data are from Experiment 3.

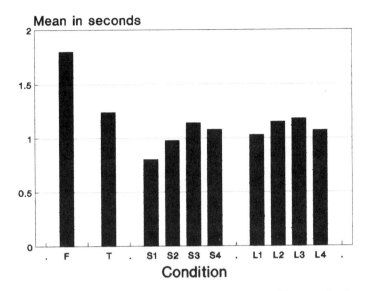

FIG. 7.4. Mean search times for the target and foil baseline conditions as well as for each similarity and location-priming condition. These data are from Experiment 4.

Discussion

Rajan stated that he used the first few digits in a cue sequence to retrieve a subset of target sequences beginning with those digits (e.g., all appropriate 10-digit blocks in the first 5,000 digits of pi) in order to determine whether any of them match the cue sequence. If his statement is correct, two results should follow: First, the similarity condition in which the first three digits of the prime are identical to the first three digits of the following target should be an effective condition for priming the target. Second, the manner in which foil sequences are constructed should be completely irrelevant because the critical point is the mismatch between the foil and the subset of target sequences retrieved. There should be no systematic differences in either errors or search time between the two types of foils generated in our experiment.

The data from these experiments support Rajan's statement. The only condition that appeared to systematically prime targets was the condition in which the first three digits of prime and target were identical. Further, there was no systematic difference between the two foil conditions in either error rate or search time.

Experiments 5–7: Similarity and Location Primes (Second 5,000 Digits)

The second 5,000 digits have been shown to be less well learned than the first 5,000 digits. Therefore, it is entirely possible that priming for targets from the second set of digits would either have different characteristics or be nonexistent. Here we report the results of priming sequences in the second 5,000 digits.

Method

The procedure, materials, and experimental design were the same as in the preceding experiments with the exception that targets were taken from the second 5,000 digits of pi and foils were taken from the first 5,000 digits.

Results

We tabulated Rajan's error rate as well as the mean search time for correct searches in each condition. As before, there were no systematic differences in either errors or search time between the two types of foils generated in these experiments so we pooled the foil data.

As in the other priming studies, we analyzed the data in two ways for each experiment. The first analysis compared unprimed targets and foils. The second analysis compared unprimed targets with targets in the eight priming conditions. All data are presented separately for each experiment.

Error Rate.   The error rate data are shown separately for each experiment in Table 7.3. These data indicated that the error rate for all conditions was extremely high in Experiment 5 but showed a systematic reduction over the next two experiments.

Mean Search Time.   The mean search times for the baseline conditions as well as each similarity and location priming condition are presented separately for each experiment in Figs. 7.5, 7.6, and 7.7. As before, trimmed means were used to compute the mean search times. The amount of data trimmed in each condition ranged from 2.5% to 12.2%. The median percentage trim was 6.0%.

TABLE 7.3
Percent Errors for Unprimed Targets, Foils, and Primed Targets in Each Similarity
and Location Condition. The Targets Are from the Second 5,000 Digits of pi

Condition	Experiment 5	Experiment 6	Experiment 7
Foil	39.8	8.5	10.6
Unprimed Target	28.6	14.8	14.5
S1	13.0	7.0	3.0
S2	19.1	15.3	10.2
S3	23.0	11.3	11.2
S4	18.0	17.0	11.1
L1	19.0	14.0	8.0
L2	25.0	14.1	11.1
L3	26.2	16.4	13.0
L4	19.1	18.0	13.8

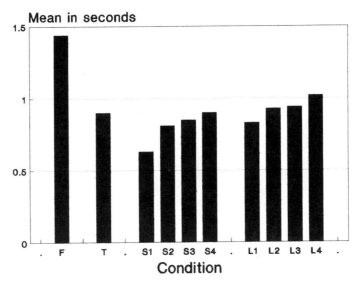

FIG. 7.5. Mean search times for the target and foil baseline conditions as well as for each similarity and location-priming condition. These data are from Experiment 5.

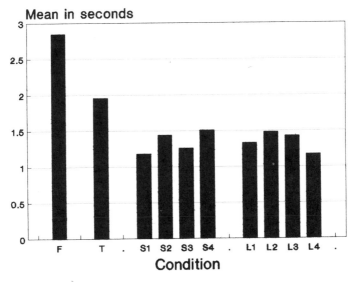

FIG. 7.6. Mean search times for the target and foil baseline conditions as well as for each similarity and location-priming condition. These data are from Experiment 6.

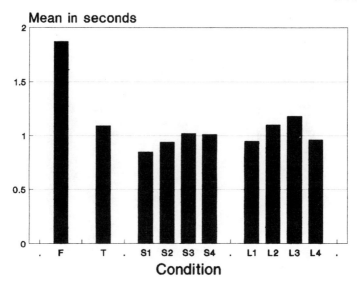

FIG. 7.7. Mean search times for the target and foil baseline conditions as well as for each similarity and location-priming condition. These data are from Experiment 7.

There is a marked difference between the target and foil in all three experiments, $F_5(1, 958) = 74.83$, MSE $= .75$, $p < .01$; $F_6(1, 1373) = 52.48$, MSE $= 3.91$, $p < .01$; $F_7(1, 1345) = 94.77$, MSE $= 1.53$, $p < .01$.

As in Experiments 3 and 4, priming systematically occurred with the S1 similarity prime in which the first three digits of the prime were the same as the first three digits of the primed target. The visual impression was confirmed by analyses, $F_5(8, 862) = 4.34$, MSE $= .23$, $p < .01$; $F_6(8, 951) = 6.99$, MSE $= 1.63$, $p < .01$; $F_7(8, 961) = 5.35$, MSE $= .19$, $p < .01$, followed by Newman–Keuls tests. Note that in the second run (i.e., Experiment 6), reliable priming occurred for all conditions.

Discussion

In chapter 5, we presented evidence that Rajan had the first 5,000 digits of pi much better learned than the second 5,000 digits. These data show one of the effects one would expect from different degrees of learning. When sequences from the second 5,000 digits were used as targets, Rajan responded to the priming task at approximately the same rate, but his error rate shot up dramatically.

As we noted previously, we grouped these data for the clearest presentation of the similarity and location prime effects. Another instructive comparison is to look at Rajan's performance on his first and second attempts at this priming task. His first attempt is designated here as Experiment 2 (where target sequences were from the first 5,000 digits of pi) and his second attempt as Experiment 5 (where target sequences were from the second 5,000 digits of pi). Rajan responded to the priming task with approximately the same speed on those two sets of trials, but his error rate quadrupled on the second attempt. Note that Rajan had the advantage of 2,400 trials on the task before beginning his second attempt.

As in the previous set of experiments, these data support Rajan's statements about his retrieval of target sequences from pi. The only condition that appeared to systematically prime targets was the condition in which the first three digits of prime and target were identical.

Experiment 8: Sequences with Three Missing Elements

The data from Experiments 2–7, together with other data from chapter 5, show that Rajan treats the 10-digit sequences of pi as chunks. He retrieves those chunks quickly and relatively accurately. One important question is to determine what information he uses to retrieve a chunk. The priming data in the previous experiments tend to support Rajan's statement that, when given a target sequence, he retrieved all relevant chunks beginning with the first few digits (e.g., 623) to check for the correct sequence. The priming data, together with his report, suggest that the first few digits in a chunk are most important, possibly critical, for retrieval of a target. This experiment used sequences with missing elements to evaluate the importance of the first few digits in the chunk for retrieval.

Method

The materials were the same as those used in the first experiment. Target and foil locations were selected as in the previous experiments: Targets were all 10 digits in a 10-digit block from the first 5,000 digits of pi, and foils were 10-digit blocks beginning at the fourth digit of a block in the second 5,000 digits of pi. All sequences had three missing digits with the locations of the missing elements randomly selected by a computer program. Except for the nature of the materials, the procedure was identical to that used in the previous experiments.

Results

We tabulated Rajan's overall error rate as well as the median search time for correct searches separately for targets and foils. In addition, we evaluated the error rate and median search time for correct responses for a number of conditions contingent on location of the missing elements.

Overall Error Rate. The error rate demonstrates that this was a very difficult task for Rajan. The error rate for foils was 8.3%, but the error rate for targets was 19.1%. Obviously, Rajan had great difficulty in identifying targets under these conditions.

Overall Median Search Time. The median search time for targets was 3.4 seconds, and the median search time for foils was 10.3 seconds. In a simple serial search model in which Rajan examines a subset of potential targets to determine whether the cue sequence is a target, the search time for foils would be double the search time for targets. Given that the median search time for foils was almost three times the median search time for targets, these data would seem to eliminate that simple serial search model.

Location-Contingent Analyses. Rajan suggested that the first three positions in a 10-digit block provide the critical cues when he searches for a block; the priming data tend to support his statement. Because the missing elements in the strings presented in this study were randomly selected, we can find strings with 0, 1, 2, or 3 of the first three digits missing. If Rajan's description were correct, we should find that increasing the number of elements missing from the first three digits in the string should have an increasingly negative effect on performance.

In sorting the data, we found that there were very few cases in which all three of the first three digits were missing from the presented string. Thus, we combined those cases with the cases in which two elements were missing from the first three digits.

Error Rate. There was no systematic change in error rate for foils as the number of missing elements in the first three digits increased. The error rate was 7.5, 9.7, and 6.0% for 0, 1, and 2 or 3 elements missing, respectively. By contrast, an increase in missing elements in the first three digits produced a dramatic increase in error rate for targets. For targets, the error rate was 4.8, 23.8, and 30.1% for 0, 1, and 2 or 3 elements missing, respectively.

These error data suggest that the critical information needed for retrieval of a 10-digit chunk (i.e., target) resides in the first three positions. As a further check of that tentative conclusion, we sorted the data for strings that had the first three digits intact but were missing either 0, 1, or 2 (or 3) elements from the next three positions in the series (i.e., Positions 4, 5, & 6). The results of that sort confirm that the critical information resides mostly in the first three elements. The error rates for strings with 0, 1, and 2 or 3 missing elements from the fourth through the sixth positions was 4.3, 9.9, and 5.0%, respectively, for foils and 2.3, 5.1, and 5.3%, respectively, for targets. The foil data was unsystematic and roughly equivalent to the data for elements missing from the first three positions.

By contrast, the target data showed systematic effects. The error rate when no elements were missing from the first six positions was half the error rate found when some elements were missing from positions four through six. Note, however, that the worst error rate for targets with elements missing in positions four through six was approximately five times better than the error rate when elements were missing from the first three positions.

Median Search Time. Unlike the error rate, the median search time changed for both targets and foils as the number of missing elements in the first three digits increased. For foils, the median search time was 4.3, 12.7, and 7.2 seconds for 0, 1, and 2 or 3 missing elements, respectively. For targets, the median search time was 1.6, 4.0, and 4.7 seconds for 0, 1, and 2 or 3 missing elements, respectively. These data show that a large increase in search time occurred with a change from no missing elements to one missing element in the first three digits. Additional elements produced no systematic change in performance.

Both the error rate and the response time data strongly suggest that the critical information needed for retrieval of a 10-digit chunk resides in the first three positions. As with the error rate data, we sorted the data for strings that had the first three digits intact but were missing either 0, 1, or 2 (or 3) elements from the next three digits in the series. The results of that sort also confirm that the critical information resides in the first three elements. The median search time for strings with 0, 1, and 2 or 3 missing elements from the fourth through the sixth digits was 2.2, 4.1, and 5.6 seconds, respectively, for foils and 1.1, 1.5, and 2.0 seconds, respectively, for targets.

Clearly, it makes little difference in the response time data whether several elements or no elements are missing from the fourth through sixth positions in the string. Sequences with missing elements in the fourth through sixth positions were identified approximately twice as rapidly as sequences with elements missing from the first three positions.

Experiment 9: Sequences With One Missing Element

All of the data thus far suggest that the first few digits in a chunk are most important to Rajan for retrieval of a target. However, in the immediately preceding study, it was difficult to assess the information carried by individual locations because all sequences had three missing digits. Thus, we decided to use sequences with one missing element to evaluate the relative importance of the first six digits in retrieving the target chunk.

Method

Targets and foils were selected as in the previous experiment. All sequences had one missing digit with the location of the missing element randomly selected from locations 1–6 by a computer program. Once again, the procedure was identical to that used in the previous experiments.

Results

We tabulated Rajan's overall error rate as well as the median search time for correct searches separately for targets and foils. In addition, we evaluated the error rate and median search time for correct responses for a number of conditions contingent on the location of the missing element.

Overall Error Rate. The error rate for foils was .9%, but the error rate for targets was 5.8%. Note that reducing the number of missing elements from three to one cut the error rate by about 75%. However, that reduction undoubtedly is an overestimate of the effect because Rajan also was increasing his skill at this task.

Overall Median Search Time. The median search time for targets was 1.8 seconds and the median search time for foils was 4.2 seconds.

Location-Contingent Analyses. This manipulation allowed us to evaluate the information carried at each location. Accordingly, we calculated the median response time for correct responses and error rate separately for each location.

Error rate. There was no systematic change in error rate for foils as a function of the location of the missing element. The error rate was 0.0, 1.2, .5, .6, .6 and 2.1% for elements missing from positions 1–6, respectively. By contrast, the location of the missing element was critical in determining error rate for targets. Given that retrieval time stays constant or increases concurrently, we assume that an increase in error rate reflects an increase in the amount of information carried by the missing element for retrieval of a 10-digit target. Error rate for targets decreased systematically over the first six digits: The error rate was 10.9, 8.5, 4.9, 6.0, 3.4 and .6% for Positions 1–6, respectively.

Median search time. Like the error rate, the median search time for foils did not change systematically with the location of the missing element. The median search time was 4.7, 4.4, 5.1, 4.1, 3.4 and 3.5 seconds for Locations 1–6, respectively. As with error rate, the time taken to retrieve targets was different from that for foils and showed the same pattern as the error rate. That is, median search time for targets decreased systematically over locations. The median search time for targets was 2.1, 2.5, 2.1, 1.7, 1.4 and 1.2 seconds for Positions 1–6, respectively.

Note that both error rate and retrieval time decrease over the first six positions in the sequence. Thus, these data do not reflect a speed–accuracy trade-off. Rather, taken together, the error rate and the response time data demonstrate that the amount of information carried for retrieval of a 10-digit chunk decreases over the first six locations in the digit sequence.

Experiment 10: Sequences With No Missing Elements

Finally, we wanted to demonstrate Rajan's performance on the task when no information was missing from the string to be evaluated. Comparison with prior experiments must be made with caution because Rajan's performance was probably still improving.

Method

The materials and procedure were the same as those used in the two previous experiments except that no digits were missing from the presented sequences.

Results

We tabulated Rajan's overall error rate as well as the median search time for correct searches separately for targets and foils.

Error Rate.   The error rate for foils was 1.1% and the error rate for targets was .8%. Note that the error rate for foils is essentially the same as in the previous experiment, but the error rate for targets has been reduced substantially through the elimination of the missing element.

Median Search Time.   The median search time for targets was 1.0 seconds and the median search time for foils was 1.4 seconds.

GENERAL DISCUSSION

As the title of this chapter suggests, we believe that the 1,000 10-digit blocks in the first 10,000 digits of pi are part of Rajan's lexicon. There are several reasons for coming to that conclusion.

Most importantly, Rajan appears to have direct access to any subset of 10-digit blocks (e.g., the blocks beginning with 823) in a manner very similar if not identical to that proposed by researchers such as Morton (1969, 1970). Next, Rajan clearly treats the blocks as chunks even though the blocks are unrelated to other meaningful information. Finally, these data show that the 10-digit chunks can be primed by a sequence which has the same starting sequence of three digits as the target sequence. In other words, Rajan responds to this conceptually barren material in much the same way as we respond to meaningful words. These chunks appear to be just as much a part of his lexicon as are uncommon words. We consider these data important because the notion that lexical entries have meaning seems to be implicit in most definitions of the lexicon. We believe these data emphasize that lexical entries can be void of meaning and can come about as a result of sheer rote learning.

We can make our point more specific by noting that Rajan's 10-digit chunks would appear to have all the characteristics of Morton's logogen even though, as we stated earlier, Morton (1970) defined a logogen "in terms of the usual understanding of 'word.' " We certainly agree that meaning and meaningful relationships play a powerful role in cognitive processes. Nevertheless, we also think the efficacy of rote learning has been consistently underestimated when discussing such concepts as chunking or logogens. These data from Rajan tend to underscore that point.

Some comparisons with standard lexical decision tasks are worth noting. The usual reaction time to single unprimed words in a lexical decision task is around 600 milliseconds with an error rate of around 3% (e.g., Neely, 1976). If we focus on the first 5,000 digits of pi, Rajan's reaction time to unprimed targets was about 1,000 milliseconds with an error rate of around 8%. That performance compares quite favorably to a slightly more difficult lexical decision task in which subjects had to decide whether both presented strings were words (Meyer & Schvaneveldt, 1971). When the two strings were unrelated words, subjects' response times were about 900 milliseconds and their error rates were about 9%.

The last three experiments presented in this chapter point out that the first three digits of the 10-digit chunk carry most of the information for access to that chunk. That makes sense on purely logical grounds. There are 1,000 10-digit chunks in the set of digits with which Rajan is most familiar (i.e., the first 10,000 digits of pi). Given any one of the 10 digits (0–9), one would expect to find approximately 100 of the 1,000 blocks beginning with that digit. Similarly, given any sequence of two digits, one would expect to find approximately 10 blocks beginning with that sequence. However, given any sequence of three digits, one would expect that 3-digit sequence typically to be the beginning sequence for a single block of the 1,000 available blocks. In short, given the size of the search set, identifying blocks by their initial 3-digit sequence is almost equivalent to using direct access. (It is "almost" equivalent rather than equivalent because there are some 3-digit sequences which appear as the beginning of more than one 10-digit block.) The strategy should produce rapid and accurate retrieval—and it did.

When we had Rajan search for digits at specified location in the pi series, he claimed to go directly to the correct row and then search the row for the digit at the specified location. Analyses of his search data were completely consistent with his claim. In these priming tasks, Rajan claimed that he retrieved all relevant chunks beginning with a particular sequence (e.g., 482). Interestingly, he always gave a 3-digit sequence as an example. As described previously, that is virtually equivalent to direct access to the target string. The data showing that the first three digits carry most of the information are certainly consistent with Rajan's claim. Given the accuracy of Rajan's description of his procedure for retrieving digits at specific locations, we are inclined to believe his description of his procedure for retrieving 10-digit chunks.

Comparison With Other Memorists

In the first chapter of this book, we described Rajan's recitation of the first 31,811 digits of pi from memory in 1981 to enter the *Guinness Book of World Records*. We also noted that Hideaki Tomoyori broke Rajan's record in 1987 by reciting the first 40,000 digits of pi. Although feats like these are rare, there have been several published accounts of people with prodigious skilled memories.

Starting with the pioneering work of Binet in 1894, the scientific literature describes over a dozen people showing exceptional memory for verbal materials. Not many years ago, Brown and Deffenbacher (1975, 1988) provided excellent and comprehensive reviews of this literature. We summarize the performance of those memorists and compare Rajan to them. Our comparisons focus entirely on performance with digits because Rajan's performance on other verbal materials is unexceptional.

MEMORISTS

We comment on the following thirteen memorists in the order in which they were investigated: Inaudi, Diamandi, Arnould, Rückle, Bergh, Isihara, Finkelstein, Shereshevskii, Aitken, V.P., S.F and D.D., and T.E. We add a recent description of "Bubbles P." (Ceci, DeSimone, & Johnson, 1993) to complete the set of investigations of memorists.

Inaudi. Inaudi was one of three memorists investigated by Binet (1894; see Brown & Deffenbacher, 1975, 1988); the other two were Diamandi and Arnould. Like Rajan, Inaudi's memory for materials other than digits was unremarkable.

125

This suggests that he had developed his skill at memorizing numbers. The procedure Inaudi used to remember digits is not described in detail other than to say he claimed to rely on auditory imagery and not a mnemonic system. With a presentation rate of one digit per second, his memory span was 25. Because Inaudi was a stage performer, we can reasonably infer his span had increased as a result of practice. He took about 7 seconds per digit to learn 100 digits compared to Rajan's 3.1 seconds per digit.

Diamandi. Diamandi was a mental calculator like Inaudi. His performance on materials other than digits was also unremarkable. He claimed not to use a mnemonic system but to rely on vivid imagery, visualizing the digits to be memorized (or calculated) in his own handwriting. Among the memorists considered here, he was relatively slow in learning digit strings. For example, he took 180 seconds to learn a 5 × 5 matrix (7.2 seconds per digit). For comparison, Rajan learned a 5 × 5 matrix at a rate of 2.1 seconds per digit.

Arnould. Binet studied Arnould as a comparison subject to Inaudi and Diamandi because Arnould used a mnemonic to memorize strings of digits. His procedure involved substituting consonants for digits using a systematic scheme (e.g., 1 = *t,d*; 2 = *n*; 3 = *m*; 4 = *r*; 5 = *l*, etc.). Words are then constructed by adding vowels where necessary. Using the substitute system given as an example, the digit string 3152 could be encoded as "a *mad loon*" or the string 1234 could be encoded as "a *ton* or *more.*" Arnould's unaided memory span was completely normal at seven digits. (Unfortunately, Binet did not test Arnould on nonnumerical materials.) Using his system, it took Arnould 13.5 seconds per digit to learn a 200-digit string. Rajan learned a 14 × 14 matrix (196 digits) at the rate of 4.3 seconds per digit. It would appear that Rajan's performance is better although we assume that the organization of a matrix produces faster learning than occurs with a comparable digit string.

Rückle. The fourth memorist to be studied was Rückle (Müller, 1911; see Brown & Deffenbacher, 1975, 1988). Unlike the others, Rückle clearly had above-average abilities with other materials as he subsequently earned a PhD in mathematics from Göttingen. He used detailed visual imagery for most of his memorization but, when learning strings of numbers, relied on his knowledge of their relationships and their characteristics.

The tests of Rückle's memory span involved a variety of procedures. The digits were presented at roughly one per second and were either presented singly or grouped in sets of five or six. When the digits were presented singly, Rückle's memory span was about 18. Rückle was tested extensively, and both his memory span and his performance on learning digit strings improved substantially. His memory span at last testing was about 60. This marked improvement in performance anticipated the later work of Chase and Ericsson (e.g., Chase & Ericsson, 1981, 1982; Ericsson & Chase, 1982). Initial tests of Rückle's ability to learn digit strings showed that he took 2.6 seconds per digit to learn 102 digits. In later tests, he reduced that time to 1.5 seconds per digit. By comparison, Rajan takes 3.1 seconds to learn a 10 × 10 matrix. In short, the initial, as well as later, tests suggest that Rückle had a longer memory span and learned digit strings faster than Rajan learned comparable matrices.

Bergh. Bergh was studied by the Norwegian philogist Hegge (1918; see Brown & Deffenbacher, 1975, 1988). Bergh used a mnemonic system, which was a version of the classic method of loci. When she memorized digits, she first converted them to objects or persons and then placed their images in order on a mental landscape. Although she could learn very long strings in this manner, she was quite slow. For example, she took 15.3 seconds per digit to learn a 408-digit string. Rajan learned a 20 × 20 matrix at the rate of 5.8 seconds per digit. Again, the comparison is approximate because the digits are presented differently (matrix vs. string), but despite this difference Rajan appears to perform better.

Finkelstein. The major studies on the memorist Finkelstein were performed by Sandor (1932) and Weinland (1948). Finkelstein claimed that he relied on his knowledge of the properties of numbers together with vivid visual imagery. Like Diamandi, he visualized the numbers written in his own handwriting on a mental blackboard; however, he also neatly grouped the digits in rows of six digits. To the best of our knowledge, there were no attempts to test his claim of visual imagery.

It is not possible to compare his digit span with any other memorist because he refused to be tested in the usual way; his digit span would obviously be quite long because he was able to recite strings of 25 or 26 digits after an exposure of only one second (Weinland, 1948). However, his time per digit increased considerably as the number of digits increased. For example, the Weinland experiments also showed that it took him 4.7 seconds per digit to learn a 4 × 18 matrix (72 digits). By contrast, Rajan took 2.7 seconds per digit to learn a 9 × 9 matrix (81 digits).

Isihara. Susukita (1933, 1934) studied the stage memorist Isihara. Isihara worked very effectively and quickly with a modification of the digit–consonant mnemonic. He converted the digits directly into syllables, recoded the syllables into words, and then used the classic method of loci to remember the words. Using this procedure, Isihara once learned 2,400 digits in 4 hours and recited them with 99.7% accuracy.

Isihara took 1.1 seconds per digit to learn a 102-digit string (Susukita, 1933). Thus, his learning rate was more than twice as fast as Rajan's.

Professor Aitken.   Perhaps the most interesting and capable memorist was described by Hunter (1977). Aitken was a brilliant mathematician, an excellent mental calculator, and an accomplished violinist with an extraordinary memory. His primary method for learning was to search out meaningful relationships within the material and with previously learned information. It is not clear how he applied his primary method to learning digits.

Aitken's digit span, initially tested with a presentation rate of two digits per second, was 13 for auditory presentation and 15 for visual presentation. Rajan produced a memory span of 15 when he was initially tested with auditory presentation at a presentation rate of one digit per second (Hanson, 1980; Horn, 1981). Given that both memorists preferred a more rapid presentation rate, the two spans are probably roughly equivalent.

Aitken learned 16 three-digit numbers, a total of 48 digits, in 128 seconds. Ignoring the advantage of grouping the digits, the per-digit rate is 2.7 seconds — that is exactly the same as Rajan's rate for learning 49 (ungrouped) digits.

Based on this limited comparison, Rajan and Professor Aitken were evenly matched in learning rate and memory span. However, the data suggest that Aitken was far superior in long-term retention. In an unexpected recall, Aitken correctly recalled 9 of the 16 groups after 28 years. As our experiments in chapter 4 show, if Rajan did not anticipate recall, he could not recall material after two months.

Shereshevskii.   Luria (1968) made Shereshevskii (S) the world's most famous memorist. His studies of Shereshevskii continued for almost 30 years. Surprisingly, Shereshevskii was unaware that his memory was unusual until Luria began his investigations.

Shereshevskii used three basic processes for remembering verbal material. The first was to generate rich visual images. Shereshevskii claimed to reproduce tables of numbers in this manner. He claimed that he continued to "see" the table which had been written on the blackboard or on a piece of paper (Luria, 1968, p. 20). However, some of the data that Luria presents appears to contradict his claim, but the data are difficult to interpret because no information is given about the number or order of tests on a matrix.

With that caveat, the data presented on page 18 of Luria's book show that Shereshevskii could reproduce all 50 digits at the rate of .8 seconds per digit. He slowed down by a factor of approximately two when producing the second column with a rate of 1.9 seconds per digit. Finally, his rate was almost eight times as slow when reproducing the third column (6.2 seconds per digit). As we argued when presenting similar data for Rajan, reading rates for rows and columns should be approximately equivalent if the subject is reading from a strong visual image. Although Luria appears to accept Shereshevskii's claim of visual imagery, we think the data just described strongly contradicts that claim with regard to matrix learning.

Rajan learned and recited number matrices much faster than Shereshevskii. For example, Rajan learned a number matrix of 49 digits at a rate of 1.7 seconds per digit which is roughly twice as fast as Shereshevskii's rate of 3.0 seconds per digit. Rajan was also twice as fast at reproducing columns from a matrix. He took 3.1 seconds per digit to reproduce the third column of a 12 × 12 matrix compared to Shereshevskii's 6.2 seconds per digit to reproduce the third column of a 4 × 13 matrix (with only 12 digits in the first and last columns).

The second process used by Shereshevskii was to create a story with appropriate images to retrieve the information. Luria describes one instance in which Shereshevskii used a story with strong visual imagery to remember a complicated mathematical formula. He apparently was able to reproduce the formula without error 15 years later although Luria's description of S's performance is ambiguous ("he was still able to trace his pattern of recall in precise detail," 1968, p. 51). Shereshevskii's long-term retention was obviously superior to Rajan's.

The third process was to mentally place images in familiar locations for later retrieval. This procedure is the method of locations (or loci) developed by the Greek poet Simonides of Ceos about 500 B.C. — Shereshevskii apparently developed it independently. Luria does not report any instance in which Shereshevskii used this process to remember digits.

In addition to these three processes, Shereshevskii had strong synesthesia; this appears to be unique among the memorists who have been investigated. Synesthesia is said to occur when information coming into one sensory system (e.g., audition) produces an effect in another sensory system (e.g., vision). Shereshevskii once said to the Russian psychologist Vygotsky, "What a crumbly, yellow voice you have" (Luria, 1968, p. 24). Similarly, Shereshevskii claimed that each number had a distinctive characteristic (e.g., "eight somehow has a naive quality, it's milky blue like lime," p. 26). While that description is most interesting, Luria provides no data to support the efficacy of the synesthetic qualities of numbers as mnemonic aids for Shereshevskii. We saw no evidence of synesthesia in Rajan.

VP. Shortly after the appearance of Luria's book on Shereshevskii, Hunt and Love (1972) performed what is arguably the most systematic and analytic study of a memorist to date. Coincidentally, their memorist grew up in a Latvian city near where Shereshevskii had been raised. VP was an only child in an intellectual family and was quite precocious. He began reading at age 3½, memorized the street map of a moderately large city by age 5, and memorized 150 poems for a contest by age 10.

VP learned material by relating it to prior information: He knew several languages and could associate any three-letter string with a word from one of those languages. He learned number matrices by rows and sometimes recoded the row as a date. It is also clear that he spent a great deal of time practicing memorizing so that he became very adept at recoding information. He learned strings of digits by blocking them in subsets ranging in length from three to five digits and associating dates, distances, ages, and arithmetic relationships to those shorter strings.

VP's initial digit span was measured at the typical rate of one digit per second. His span was about eight, which is unremarkable. He was tested on the 50-digit matrix learned by Shereshevskii and took 390 seconds to learn it (7.8 seconds per digit). That is twice as long as Shereshevskii and over four times as long as Rajan.

SF and DD.   In a number of published reports (Chase & Ericsson, 1981, 1982; Ericsson & Chase, 1982; Ericsson, Chase, & Faloon, 1980), Ericsson and Chase demonstrated that a skilled memory can be developed with massive amounts of practice. Both SF and DD began with ordinary memory spans of around seven digits. After 200–300 hours of practice at the memory span task, they both developed spans exceeding 70 digits.

Both SF and DD took about the same time to learn Luria's matrix on their first attempt (3.7 and 3.9 seconds per digit). These times were much slower than Rajan's time on a comparable matrix (1.7 seconds per digit). However, after 1 year of practice on the task, SF learned at approximately the same rate as Rajan (1.6 seconds per digit).

TE.   The most recent published study of a memorist at the time this book was written was by Gordon, Valentine, and Wilding (1984). TE worked as a civil servant in England. His performance was unremarkable until he began to develop his mnemonic abilities around age 15. He remembered numbers using a version of the digit–consonant substitution procedure described earlier. When learning matrices, he elaborated the procedure using a combination of a peg-list and chain systems: Each row is represented by a picture previously assigned to single digits. For example, the first row is represented by "eat." TE split the six numbers in each row into two sets and generated a word for each set. He then associated the words in the first row with locations in a canteen with which he is familiar.

Based on the mean of five trials, TE had a memory span of 12. He learned the 50-digit Luria matrix in 144 seconds (2.9 seconds per digit). That was very good performance but not as fast as Rajan. Like the other memorists, TE took longer to retrieve the third column of the matrix (72.2 seconds) than to retrieve the second column (43.2 seconds).

Bubbles P.   The most recent investigation of a memorist (excluding Rajan) was that on "Bubbles P." (Ceci, DeSimone, & Johnson, 1993). Bubbles earned his living as a professional gambler and was 33 years old at the time his memory was tested. (Bubbles and Rajan are about the same age.) Bubbles had a memory span of 15–20 digits. What is interesting and unusual is that he had the same memory span whether he was asked to recall the digits in order of presentation or in backward order. The memory span of a normal adult subject is halved when they are required to recall the digits in reverse order. Although we made no formal tests of Rajan's backward span, he voluntarily produced digit strings in both orders on several occasions. Our impression was that he could do both orders equally well.

Bubbles was tested on the 50-digit matrix learned by Shereshevskii. He took 424 seconds to learn the matrix (8.5 seconds per digit), which was slower than either VP or Shereshevskii and much slower than Rajan. Once the matrix was learned, Bubbles claimed to have a strong visual image of the matrix. Informal reports of his performance supported his statement as he was said to be able to give the number at a specified location very quickly.

However, the data presented on his performance were not entirely consistent with that interpretation. Most importantly, he took 50.6 seconds to report the third column of the Luria matrix but only 35.5 seconds to report the second column. This pattern suggests that he had to search each row and read out the digit from the appropriate column—rather than read directly from a visual image. For comparison, VP took 58.1 seconds to read out the third column and Shereshevskii took 80 seconds on the same task. Rajan took 36.8 seconds to read out the third column in a 12 × 12 matrix. It would appear that Bubbles could report the matrix much faster than Shereshevskii and slightly faster than VP, but he was much slower than Rajan.

Bubbles appeared to be very like Rajan in that he used no obvious mnemonics or recoding strategies to learn digit strings. He did claim to regroup a string of digits into 2s, 3s, or 4s when the digits were first presented to him. Like Rajan, he seemed to encode the location of the digits in the string.

Also like Rajan, his skill was limited to tests with digits as well as tests that appeared to be related to his gambling activities. He was very good at recognizing faces and exceptionally good at recalling matrices of cards. On other tests, he was unexceptional.

RECAPITULATION

When we consider only performance on digit strings, Rajan is superior to 10 of the 13 memorists studied. His learning rate is inferior to Rückle and Isihara, and his long-term retention is inferior to Professor Aitken.

The two best-known memorists, Shereshevskii and VP, were inferior to Rajan in learning digit strings. However, it is clear that they were more versatile in what they could learn, and they remembered that material for long periods of time. Rajan's procedure for learning was quite different from that of VP and Shereshevskii. Rajan used a procedure pairing locations and digits to learn the material. He also encoded the digits in chunks (such as a row in a matrix). Thus, he learned that the fifth digit in the fourth row was 3 rather than using preexisting knowledge to encode the information. He explicitly attached cues to the chunks for retrieval. For example, he learned the first column in a matrix as a cue for retrieving each row of the matrix.

Once the material was learned, Rajan's procedure allowed for extremely effective retrieval of information: Working in the first 10,000 decimal digits of pi, he could retrieve a digit at a specified location (e.g., digit 4,765) in an average time of 12 seconds. He had the digits of pi chunked in groups of 10 digits. When he was given the first 5 digits of a 10-digit group in the first 10,000 digits of pi, he could give the next 5 digits in an average time of 7 seconds.

Clearly, Rajan was very good at manipulating digits and exceeded most other memorists in that task. On the other hand, he was quite ordinary at nondigit tasks, but so were several other memorists (Inaudi, Diamandi, Finkelstein, SF and DD, and probably Arnould).

We close this section with a comment on what became a rather striking observation to us. When making these comparisons, we noted that investigators often accepted memorists' introspections about their processing even when the data contradicted those explanations. We can appreciate that the performance of a memorist can be so dazzling that the temptation to take his or her personal testimony at face value is very strong. In our investigations, we took the view that Rajan's introspections were an interesting starting point which could be accepted only after we had reasonably strong confirmatory evidence.

THE MEMORISTS AND ERICSSON'S THEORY OF SKILLED MEMORY

As we noted earlier, Ericsson and his colleagues (e.g., Ericsson & Chase, 1982) suggest three general principles for skilled memory and illustrate these principles with people skilled at some aspect of memory. The three principles they propose are meaningful encoding (the use of preexisting knowledge to store the presented information in memory), retrieval structure (explicitly attaching cues to the encoded material to allow efficient retrieval), and speed-up (a reduction in study time with further practice). They claim that ordinary subjects, as well as skilled memorists, show these principles.

As an initial test of their theory, consider four of the memorists for which we have considerable data: Professor Aitken, Shereshevskii, VP, and Rajan. Consistent with the Ericsson and Chase theory, all four memorists attached retrieval cues when learning material (retrieval structure) to ensure accurate and fast retrieval, and three of them showed a reduction in study time with practice (speed-up). There was no clear evidence available on this point for Professor Aitken; however, it seems likely that he would show a similar effect.

The data from these memorists suggest that the skilled memory theory founders on Ericsson and Chase's principle of meaningful encoding. Certainly, all four memorists used procedures for encoding the material that are available to, and used by, people with ordinary memories. But, contrary to the theory, only some of them encoded the material by relating it to preexisting knowledge. VP fits the theory because he encoded material by relating it to prior information. Aitken used that technique and also searched for relationships within the material to be learned. However, Shereshevskii used imagery and the classic method of locations as his primary means for learning material. Because Ericsson and his colleagues clearly refer to relating the material to preexisting verbal knowledge, Shereshevskii's procedures, being visual, at best only weakly conform to their theory. Rajan, on the other hand, does not fit the theory at all. His procedure, pairing locations and digits, cannot be construed as encoding by relation to preexisting knowledge.

Finally, Ericsson and Chase are adamant in insisting that, with adequate practice, any normal person can achieve the performance demonstrated by these memorists. We believe they are partially correct: Ordinary people can achieve performance which is mind-boggling to those who do not understand the basis of that performance. Their subject, SF, stands as a prime example as his memory span performance ultimately exceeded 80 digits. However, we also believe their basic assertion to be false. Practice as long as we could and try as hard as we might, most of us will never be able to dribble and shoot with the skill, speed, and accuracy of a professional soccer or basketball player. They begin with a basic physical ability which far exceeds our own. There is no reason why we should expect any difference in the mental realm. Given all the practice possible, we do not believe a normal adult could reach the performance of a Shereshevskii or a Professor Aitken—or a Rajan.

MOTIVATION: THE WHY QUESTION

Most of the memorists we have described learned large quantities of generally useless material. That observation leads one to wonder about the motivation for such learning. Indeed, one of the most common questions we are asked about Rajan is, "Why did he ever bother to learn 35,000 digits of pi?"

We cannot speak in detail about the motivation of the other memorists described in this chapter, but we had very close contact with Rajan for about 3 years, and we came to know him very well. Thus, although we can provide no direct evidence to answer that question, we believe we can speculate somewhat intelligently about his motivation to undertake such a task.

Questions of motivation are difficult to address, particularly when asked about individual behavior. Motivation can be extrinsic or intrinsic. Voting to acquire a button proclaiming the fact, and presumably winning the admiration of friends, is extrinsic. Voting out of a sense of duty that accompanies the privilege of citizenship is intrinsic. Voting to proclaim the right of grumbling about those in office is probably somewhere in between.

It is likely that Jedediah Buxton, a famous calculating prodigy (Ball, 1956), was intrinsically driven: When given the size of an object he would immediately and without prodding set out to compute the number of hair-breadths it contained, sometimes breaking off the calculation to do other things and picking up where he left off 2 weeks later. Chase and Ericsson's subject (SF) presumably was extrinsically motivated by the money he was paid. Ericsson, Krampe, and Tesch-Romer (1989) claimed that, given a population of talented musicians, the factor separating the truly successful from the also-rans is the time put into practice. Are the hours spent a result of a heightened degree of enjoyment not shared by musicians who are merely "good"? Or is it the promise of a lucrative career? It may be difficult for some to believe that so much work is expended for a reward that is so distant, or worse, a mere promise.

Luria virtually ignored this problem except for a brief discussion of Shereshevskii's problem of being unable to forget. Luria avoided the question of whether Shereshevskii was driven to remember or if it was an effortless task; the latter was implied. We can sympathize with Luria somewhat. When one is seized with the fascination of awe-inspiring performance, one ignores such questions. So it was with us.

Even if we cannot resolve the issue, we at least know that extrinsic factors were a strong motivating force in Rajan's case. A review of the first chapter attests to this. He took great delight in displaying his prowess at the local bars and coffee house, and not even painful cracked ribs could keep him from a classroom demonstration. There is no evidence that Rajan was driven like Buxton who unhesitatingly turned sermons into word counts (considered by some to be a prudent use of his time). If Rajan was driven, then he would have rehearsed all those matrices which he thought would not be retested.

It is safe to say that throughout Rajan's life praise for displays of memory were often and immediate, and this causes us to lean toward the belief that his motivations were extrinsic. We are cautioned, however, by the knowledge that the answers to such complex questions are rarely so simple. We have scant information about his childhood years when he may indeed have been driven by his fascination with his own memory.

Overview and Interpretation
of Rajan's Performance

The studies reported in this book provide additional information on the characteristics of expert memory. Our data show the retrieval strategies of an expert memorist performing several tasks with digit strings. In this chapter, we summarize the important points that we think emerged from these data. Then we discuss how Rajan's performance fits with Ericsson's theory of skilled memory. Finally, we question whether Rajan's ability should be viewed as resulting from great talent or extensive practice.

Although the data reported here focus on the performance of a single memorist, we believe they have broader significance for several reasons. The two most important are that these data show beyond any reasonable doubt that Rajan has chunked the digits of pi by rote learning, and they show the characteristics of retrieval from a very large well-defined memory set.

CHUNKS PRODUCED BY ROTE LEARNING

When researchers discuss chunking, they invariably emphasize the meaning that is typically attached to chunks. We certainly agree that meaning and meaningful relationships play a powerful role in cognitive processes. Nevertheless, we also think the efficacy of rote learning has been consistently underestimated when discussing such concepts as chunking or logogens. These data from Rajan tend to underscore that point. More specifically, Rajan's 10-digit chunks are almost totally bereft of relationships to meaningful material. Nevertheless, they have all the characteristics of Morton's logogen even though Morton (1970) defined a logogen "in terms of the usual understanding of 'word' " (p. 206).

Virtually all of our data dealing with Rajan's retrieval of the digits of pi point to the psychological reality of his 10-digit chunk. First, most of his errors when retrieving digits at specific locations were errors in which he had the correct location within a 10-digit block but was searching the wrong 10-digit block. Second, give Rajan the first 5 digits of a 10-digit block, and he can retrieve the following 5 digits with considerable speed and accuracy. In contrast, he is very slow at retrieving subsequent digits if the 5-digit sequence is buried within a 10-digit block. Indeed, he often fails in the task.

We think some of the most convincing evidence for the psychological reality of Rajan's 10-digit chunk is his ability to quickly (and fairly reliably) discriminate between targets (sequences beginning 10-digit chunks) and foils in a lexical decision task. Rajan appears to have direct access to any subset of 10-digit blocks (e.g., the blocks beginning with 823) in a manner very similar if not identical to that proposed by researchers such as Morton (1969, 1970). In addition, he clearly treats the blocks as chunks even though the blocks are unrelated to other meaningful information.

Finally, the 10-digit chunks can be primed by a sequence that has the same starting sequence of three digits as the target sequence. In other words, Rajan responds to this conceptually barren material in much the same way as we respond to meaningful words. These chunks appear to be just as much a part of his lexicon as are uncommon words. That is an important point because the notion that lexical entries have meaning seems to be implicit in most definitions of the lexicon. We believe Rajan's performance shows that lexical entries can be void of meaning. It is clear that some of Rajan's entries (his 10-digit chunks) came about as a result of sheer rote learning.

When discussing chunking, researchers (e.g., Egan & Schwarz, 1979; Vicente, 1988) suggested that chunks can be classified as either perceptual or conceptual. Vicente concluded that there were four conditions under which chunks could be formed. He states:

> There are four logical possibilities. First, there is the case where chunks are meaningful to the observer but are easily perceived because they are associated with a given perceptual pattern. Second, there is the case where the chunks are not meaningful but are nevertheless easily perceived via their perceptual characteristics. This instance is a type of rote learning where the subject recognizes the stimulus via its syntactic properties, but does not have an understanding of the underlying semantics. While logically distinct, both of these types of chunking are subsumed by the perceptual account. A third type of chunking can take place when the stimulus is familiar in the sense that it has been encountered before but is not tied to a specific perceptual configuration. Finally, the fourth type of chunking occurs when the stimulus has never been encountered before (i.e., it is unfamiliar) but, nevertheless, is meaningful to the domain expert. Both of these

last two types of chunking are subsumed by the conceptual account of chunking. (p. 263)

We suggest that Rajan's digit groups do not fall under any of the four categories described by Vicente: Whereas Vicente's initial description of the second perceptual category suggests that it is appropriate for Rajan's 10-digit chunks, the next sentence, emphasizing syntax and semantics, makes it clear that Rajan's chunks do not fit that category. They can be regarded as perceptual units, but they do not have syntactic or semantic properties. Thus, Rajan's 10-digit chunks make an important point in a somewhat dramatic fashion. Chunks can be formed which are perceptual (i.e., the blocks of 10 digits are automatically perceived as a block) but have no meaning. Nevertheless, those chunks are directly retrievable in a manner analogous to the retrieval of familiar words or scenes.

Although Rajan's chunks are unusual, they are based on perceptual grouping. The effectiveness of perceptual grouping in producing chunks is not new. This was pointed out first by the Gestalt psychologists and, more recently, discussed in detail by Bower (1972). He pointed out that grouping could be accomplished by color, visual or auditory gaps, and other perceptual markers (e.g., zeroes in a string of digits). In short, it is very easy to produce a perceptual marker to place items into groups. When Rajan began to learn the digits of pi, his source material provided rows and spaces between successive groups of 10 digits, which visually highlighted the to-be-learned chunk.

RAJAN'S RETRIEVAL STRATEGIES IN A LARGE, WELL-DEFINED MEMORY SET

A portion of the data presented in this book are truly unique. They represent the only data from experiments in which memory searches have been done in a very large, exactly defined set of materials (the first 10,000 decimal digits of pi). In addition, the organization in memory of this large set can be clearly inferred. There are a large number of studies investigating memory search in well-defined memory sets in both short-term (e.g., Sternberg, 1966) and long-term memory (e.g., Atkinson & Juola, 1974; Corballis, Katz, & Schwartz, 1980). To the best of our knowledge, the largest set of items used in such experiments was 32 words (Atkinson & Juola, 1974).

We think it is of some interest to examine the strategies used for retrieving items from a set that is over 300 times the size of the largest set previously examined. In fact, Rajan's retrieval strategies depend on the task he is given. He uses several task-dependent strategies when working with a large memory set. We have organized those strategies in terms of the cues that are available to Rajan in the task. We also take this opportunity to emphasize a strategy he *does not* use. Because people observing Rajan's performance typically conclude that he must have a "photographic memory," we begin with the evidence showing that he does not use imagery for recall.

Rajan Does Not Have a "Photographic" Memory

We assume that those observers who conclude that Rajan has a photographic memory are assuming that he recalls from a visual image. There are a number of lines of converging evidence showing that he does not use visual imagery in recall. We can begin with his personal claim that he does not use imagery. Add to that the evidence from our studies (reported in chapter 3), those by Baddeley (Baddeley, Mahadevan, & Thompson, 1992), and by Biederman (Biederman, Cooper, Fox, & Mahadevan, 1992), all of which show that Rajan's performance is, at best, average on tests which appear to involve visual imagery.

But the most convincing evidence of all, in our opinion, is his performance during recall of matrices. Rajan retrieves every row of a matrix with equal speed. However, his retrieval time varies widely for columns. He takes much longer to retrieve interior columns than exterior (e.g., first and last) columns. Only the first column is retrieved as rapidly as the rows. It seems fairly obvious that, if Rajan were reading from a clear visual image, his time to retrieve rows and columns should be approximately equal. One could argue that it might take a bit longer to determine which column to read than it took to determine which row to read. However, that difference would be quite small, whereas the differences that Rajan shows when retrieving rows and columns are very large. In short, all the evidence converges to say that Rajan is correct when he claims that he does not use visual imagery.

Rajan's 10-Digit Chunks

Several bits of evidence point to the psychological reality of Rajan's 10-digit chunks, with the priming experiments providing the most convincing evidence. In a number of studies, we gave Rajan a fragment of a 10-digit chunk (or a foil fragment) and asked him to respond by indicating whether the fragment could be completed as a 10-digit chunk in a 5,000-digit subset of the first 10,000 digits. Rajan responded quite rapidly and reasonably accurately as the targets and foils were presented. Priming occurred when a foil presented just before the target began with the same three digits (in the same order) as the target. Later experiments showed that most of the information about the 10-digit chunk is carried in the first three digits. Put differently, Rajan had the hardest time completing a fragment of a chunk when those three digits were omitted.

In the priming experiments, it is obvious that Rajan was responding to the fragments of a 10-digit chunk in a way that at least is very similar to, and probably identical to, the way people respond to word fragments. Lexical decision is performed with whole words and not word fragments. We suspect that people presented with word fragments would do no better than Rajan did on this task.

Location Cues

Our studies show that Rajan has the digits of pi stored in memory in exactly the way they are presented in his source material. The source presents them in rows of 100 digits, and each row is divided into 10 blocks of 10 digits each. He retrieves individual numbers from specific locations in the first 10,000 digits of pi by retrieving the correct row very rapidly (in about 1.5 seconds) and then "counting over" to the correct location. Because our data establish that Rajan has chunked the 10-digit blocks in the row, we speculate that Rajan's counting over consists of first finding the correct chunk of 10 digits and then finding the digit at the correct location within that chunk.

Rajan also makes extensive use of location cues in matrix learning and in the memory span task. In both cases, the evidence suggests that he uses a modified paired-associate (cue–target) procedure in which the cue is the location of the digit and the target is the digit to be learned. We call it a modified paired-associate procedure because Rajan divides the series of digits into chunks in both memory span and matrix learning. The chunk in matrix learning is the row, and Rajan learns the first column as an aid for keeping the rows straight. Then, within each row, Rajan applies the paired-associate procedure we have described.

In the memory span task, Rajan divides the series into chunks which usually vary in size from 13 to 17 digits. The digits within the chunks are then learned by position using the paired-associate procedure.

We informally observed another strategy. In some memory span tests, Rajan would lose two, three, or four items in the middle of one of his chunks and then do a serial search (i.e., systematically go through all the possibilities) for those items. Three things were interesting about those occasions: (a) There seemed to be a serial position effect (i.e., the lost items were in the middle of the sequence), (b) Rajan was able to hold all the other digits in mind while he engaged in the serial search (suggesting storage in long-term memory), and (c) he was often able to recognize the correct missing elements, suggesting some sort of memory trace that was not adequate for recall but was sufficient for recognition. Although we found these instances quite fascinating, we did not attempt to document them; that was probably a mistake. We thought, when we first observed Rajan engage in this behavior, that we could not collect enough instances to be convincing. After the fact, we are less sure that we made the correct decision.

VISUAL SEARCH IN THE FIRST 20,000 DIGITS OF PI

When Rajan searched for digits at specific locations in a visual display of 20,000 digits, his performance was virtually identical to that of the control subjects. He and the control subjects began by locating the correct page (of four pages) and then searched for the correct 1,000 block within that page. Having found the correct 1,000 block, they proceeded to find the appropriate row (100 block), the appropriate block of 10 within the row, and the appropriate digit within the block of 10.

Finally, there was a residual time which we assumed to be encoding/production time. That time included the time to read and interpret the location to be found as well as the time to read and produce the digit at the target location. We created a linear model for this search process. When the data were sorted into the hypothesized components, Rajan and the control subjects showed the same pattern of responding.

Most importantly, our analyses showed that Rajan's memory search data did not fit the pattern just described. An attempt to analyze the data into the components just described produced a negative encoding/production time. That result has two implications: First, the theoretical structure we created for visual search is falsifiable—a necessary condition for an adequate theoretical proposal. Second, Rajan's visual and memory search used different strategies.

The last point to be made about his visual search is that it appears not to be compatible with his memory search. Rajan reported that he initially tried memory search as an aid to visual search. He claimed the memory search interfered with his visual search. If Rajan used visual imagery in memory search, one might reasonably expect memory search to facilitate visual search.

MATRIX LEARNING:
LONG-TERM RETENTION AND REHEARSAL

Our data demonstrates that Rajan does not remember unless he rehearses. More specifically, our experiments led us to three conclusions: First, his performance on the initial matrices showed that he could maintain outstanding performance on number sets with some rehearsal. The fact that he did not show equally impressive performance on retention tests for the second and third matrix sets strongly suggests that he had not rehearsed those sets. Our interpretation is further supported by the observation that he was unable to recall any of the matrices from the first set after 1 year even though he recalled some of the Minnesota matrices after 8½ years. The pattern of performance suggests that his long-term retention of some of the matrices in our initial study as well as some of the Minnesota matrices resulted from rehearsal of those matrices.

Second, we argue that Rajan's performance on the new matrices in the second and third matrix sets (for which he had not anticipated memory tests) represented a test of his memory unaided by rehearsal. Those tests showed that he could not recall matrices after retention intervals of 2 or 6 months unless they have been rehearsed; however, he was able to recognize approximately two-thirds of the matrices at both retention intervals. That performance was substantially above that of the control subjects.

Third, the data also suggest Rajan did not physically record the matrices. If he had recorded them, his performance at 1 year could have been as "good" as his performance at 6 months. Rajan had a strong desire to look good on these tests, but we are quite confident that this did not extend to recording the matrices.

Rajan's long-term memory was clearly not as spectacular as the memory reported for Shereshevskii (Luria, 1968) and documented for VP (Hunt & Love, 1972). At the same time, his memory performance on matrices was substantially superior to our well-practiced control subjects. Whereas his long-term memory is poorer than either Shereshevskii or VP, his speed at learning matrices is superior to both of those memorists.

MEMORY SPAN

Rajan's memory span for numbers (60) appears to be far superior to his memory span for letters (13). Yet 13 letters certainly pushes the upper limit for "normal" spans. The observation that with longer lists there was a rehearsal time separating Rajan's first response from list offset, allowed us to distinguish normal spans from "supraspans." This provided a basis on which we might redefine memory span. It is suggested that Rajan's "true" span was indicated by the length of a continuous and rapid response stream from the last list item.

As for Rajan's encoding strategy, these tests first revealed the location association scheme. We have more to say about this in the following section.

RAJAN'S PERFORMANCE
AND ERICSSON'S SKILLED MEMORY THEORY

As described earlier, Ericsson and his colleagues (1980, 1982) proposed three general principles for skilled memory. These three principles are meaningful encoding (the use of pre-existing knowledge to encode the presented information), retrieval structure (explicitly attaching retrieval cues to the encoded material to allow efficient retrieval), and speed-up (a reduction in study time with further practice).

Rajan's performance demonstrated two of the general principles proposed by Chase and Ericsson (retrieval structure and speed-up). However, his encoding procedure does not appear to be consistent with the third principle (meaningful encoding).

We can illustrate Rajan's performance in relation to the Chase and Ericsson theory in three areas: memory span, matrix learning, and location search. Although our objective was not to test the Chase and Ericsson theory, our experiments often produced evidence relevant to it.

Memory Span

Rajan's memory span increased substantially following the initial test at the University of Minnesota (Hanson, 1980; Horn, 1981). His digit span was 15 at that time but 7 years later our tests showed that his span was around 40. After considerable additional practice on the task, Rajan could produce memory spans of around 60 digits. This increase was not surprising because Chase and Ericsson (Chase & Ericsson, 1981, 1982; Ericsson, 1985, 1988; Ericsson & Chase, 1982; Ericsson, Chase, & Faloon, 1980; Ericsson & Faivre, 1988) showed data from subjects who developed digits spans over 80 digits with the use of mnemonics and extensive practice. Rajan enjoys tasks involving numbers. Thus, it seems highly probable that he would have practiced the memory span task once he discovered it.

At the same time, his increase in digit span was not accompanied by an increase in letter span. That outcome was consistent with the results of Ericsson, Chase, and Faloon (1980) demonstrating that their memory expert (SF) also showed no transfer of his much improved digit span to a consonant memory span test.

Although his increase in span was similar to the Chase and Ericsson subjects, Rajan's procedure for encoding digit span appeared to be markedly different in two respects. First, Rajan's group size varied from 14 to 17 digits, and he did not decide in advance how to group the digits. Chase and Ericsson seem to imply that deciding grouping in advance is necessary for success.

Second, Rajan described a procedure for learning a memory span sequence that resembles paired-associate (or cue–target) learning. The correct digits were the targets and the cues were the location in the list. He kept track of the location of each digit while learning sequences of 14 to 17 digits. At the end, he connected the shorter sequences to give the complete string.

Rajan stated that he was flexible about sequence length so that he could take advantages of patterns that might occur at the end of a sequence. Our observations suggested that he used sequences ranging from 10 to 15 digits and kept track of the starting location of those sequences.

Chase and Ericsson (1981,1982) stressed that subjects achieve supraspan performance by grouping digits into chunks which can be tied to preexisting knowledge (encodable chunks). Rajan usually does not use chunking of three or four digits as a strategy. Indeed, Rajan may not recognize an encodable sequence during presentation. Further, we believe that he does not require encodable chunks for learning or retrieving a sequence.

We have pointed out that deep encoding of chunks might be demonstrated in at least two ways. There could be evidence for long-term retention of the encoded chunk or sequence, and similar sequences could interfere with one another. Data from the ascending–descending memory span study showed both the predicted retention and interference effects. Further, the specific form which interference took supported the claim that Rajan uses a system which encodes digits by location.

To repeat the example given in chapter 2, Rajan failed to recall a sequence correctly in a series of ascending spans. He pointed out that the digits in positions 10, 11, and 12 were 904 in the current series, whereas the digits in positions 10, 11, and 12 in a series four trials back were 903. He was unable to remember whether the 4 or the 3 belonged in this series. His memory for the digits and locations was completely accurate.

Rajan's performance is completely consistent with a system that encodes digits by location. In contrast, his performance is not consistent with a procedure that chunks the two sequences by relating them to preexisting knowledge. Under that procedure, the two strings would be coded as disparate events and they should not be confused with one another.

Additional evidence for the claim that Rajan encodes digits by locations comes from the same study using ascending and descending spans. We asked Rajan, without any forewarning, to recall any number segments he could remember following two experimental sessions. He identified the locations of 25 out of the 27 unique sequences produced in those recalls and made an error of only one position for the other two.

Rajan's performance in locating strings is impressive evidence for our belief that Rajan was encoding by location in a paired-associate fashion. Further support comes from the fact that it was not unusual for him to recall a sequence backward (specifying location of course). We have noted that it stretches credulity to suggest that he encoded a string by chunking according to prior knowledge and then recalled it backward.

In summary, the memory span data show the practice effects found by Chase and Ericsson. However, these data also show that an encoding/retrieval structure based on paired-associate learning, which is quite different from that which Chase and Ericsson suggest is necessary, can be equally effective.

Matrix Learning

Two of the principles proposed by Chase and Ericsson (retrieval structure and speed-up) were clearly demonstrated in the matrix studies. Because we did several sets of matrix studies, we could show that Rajan's time to learn the matrices decreased with practice. Rajan's retrieval structure was also clear. He learned each matrix by rows and could recite any row with ease without forewarning. As we have noted, he also learned the first column of the matrix as an aid to remembering the order of the rows.

Once again, however, the evidence suggested that he used his paired-associate procedure for learning the sequence of digits in a row. The main difference between his performance on memory span and his performance in learning matrices was that the size of his chunk varied in memory span, but he always selected the row as the chunk in matrix learning.

Location Search

The location search data again support the retrieval structure and speed-up principles put forth by Chase and Ericsson. The memory and retrieval structure for the first 10,000 digits of pi are made very clear by the series of studies examining Rajan's search for digit at specific locations. Rajan also speeded up with practice on that task.

Of course, Rajan came to our laboratory with those 10,000 digits of pi already well learned. We cannot state with certainty what procedure he used for learning those digits. At the same time, everything we know about Rajan suggests that his procedures were quite fixed. Recall that he used his procedures for learning number strings with strings of words (the word list studies) even when that procedure was wholly inappropriate (i.e., for the organizable lists).

Conclusion

In the areas for which we collected extensive data, Rajan's performance showed two of the three principles of skilled performance proposed by Chase and Ericsson. Rajan conformed to skilled memory theory in that he demonstrated speed-up and a clear retrieval structure.

Rajan did not conform to the third principle of skilled memory theory. None of our data suggests that he used preexisting knowledge to encode the presented material. Thus, he did not show meaningful encoding as described by Chase and Ericsson. Rather, he used a modified paired-associate procedure to learn strings of digits.

GREAT TALENT OR EXTENSIVE PRACTICE?

People observing Rajan's performance tend to assume that Rajan must have amazing ability. Another possibility has been raised by Chase and Ericsson (1981, 1982). They demonstrated that ordinary subjects can produce astounding performance after long practice. Do we attribute Rajan's performance to great talent or extensive practice?

The most relevant data to answer that question come from our studies and the studies by Baddeley (Baddeley, Mahadevan, & Thompson, 1992). The Baddeley studies used two of our (by that time) very experienced control subjects and a couple of graduate students as the control subjects. Given the nature of the control subjects, we might reasonably expect performance to be considerably better than one would find with a random sample of the population. Compared to those control subjects, Rajan's performance appeared to be average.

By the time we ran most of the nonnumerical studies with Rajan, our control subjects were also quite sophisticated. Again, compared to those controls, Rajan's performance could be described as average.

The one exception to Rajan's "average" performance is his letter span. To the best of our knowledge, he was first introduced to that task in our laboratory. As demonstrated by our tests and those of Ericsson, Chase, and Faloon (1980), letter span did not increase following a massive increase in digit span as a result of practice. Given Rajan's focus on performance with digits, we do not believe he ever practiced the letter span task. Thus, we believe that he does have a letter span of about 12 letters, which reflects unpracticed performance. Put succinctly, while he is equivalent to sophisticated subjects in most measures, his memory span appears to be at the high end of the distribution.

Although we argue that Rajan's memory span is at the high end of the distribution, it is important to point out that we do not suggest his ability is such as to put him outside the distribution. We think that we could identify a number of talented individuals who could match Rajan's performance given equivalent practice. In summary, we suggest that Rajan's performance results from a combination of extensive practice and a memory that is much better than average in certain respects.

The easiest metaphors for Rajan's performance come from the performing arts and sports. We know that, given enough practice, there are considerable number of talented individuals who could perform with top-ranked orchestras or play professional sports. At the same time, we know that most individuals could not achieve either of those goals no matter how much they practiced. They simply lack the prerequisite talent. Rajan is in the talented group. He is not unique, but he is damn good.

CONCLUDING COMMENTS

We noted in chapter 1, as performance becomes more and more skilled it becomes less and less available to conscious inspection. We were not surprised that Rajan's skilled performance had become automatic and unavailable to his inspection. We must caution that the mechanisms underlying skilled performance also become increasingly opaque to the observer as the performance becomes more skilled. Nevertheless, the evidence strongly suggests that Rajan does not seek to attach meaning to the strings he learns. He does keep track of the location of those strings in the span.

As we finish this small book, it has been more than a year since we last tested Rajan. We continue to marvel at his impressive performance. More importantly, we continue to be amazed that he could produce such outstanding performance with what seems to us to be an intellectually barren encoding procedure. The three of us came away from these experiments with a renewed appreciation of the effectiveness of rote learning. We do not think we will overlook its importance again.

References

Atkinson, R. C., & Juola, J. F. (1974). Search and decision processes in recognition memory. In D. H. Krantz, R. C. Atkinson, R. D. Luce, & P. Suppes (Eds.), *Contemporary developments in mathematical psychology* (Vol. 1, pp. 242–293). San Francisco: Freeman.

Baddeley, A. D. (1968). A three-minute reasoning task based on grammatical transformation. *Psychonomic Science, 10*, 341–342.

Baddeley, A. D. (1990). *Human memory*. Boston: Allyn & Bacon.

Baddeley, A. D. (1992). Working memory. *Science, 255*, 556–559.

Baddeley, A. D., & Hitch, G. (1974). Working memory. In G. H. Bower (Ed.), *The psychology of learning and motivation: Advances in research and theory* (Vol. 8, pp. 47–89). New York: Academic.

Baddeley, A. D., Mahadevan, R., & Thompson, C. P. (1992). *Exploring the memory of a memorist: Basic capacity or acquired expertise?* Unpublished manuscript.

Ball, W. W. R. (1956). Calculating prodigies. In J. R. Newman (Ed.), *The world of mathematics* (Vol. 1, pp. 467–487). New York: Simon & Schuster.

Bartlett, F. C. (1932). *Remembering: A study in experimental and social psychology*. London: Cambridge University Press.

Battig, W. F., & Montague, W. E. (1969). Category norms for verbal items in 56 categories: A replication and extension of the Connecticut category norms. *Journal of Experimental Psychology Monograph, 80*(3, Pt. 2).

Biederman, I., Cooper, E. E., Fox, P. W., & Mahadevan, R. S. (1992). Unexceptional spatial memory in an exceptional memorist. *Journal of Experimental Psychology: Learning, Memory, and Cognition, 18*, 654–657.

Binet, A. (1894). *Psychologie des grandes calculateurs et joueurs d'échecs* [Psychology of great calculators and chess players]. Paris: Librarie Hachette.

Bousfield, W. A. (1953). The occurrence of clustering in the recall of randomly arranged associates. *Journal of General Psychology, 49*, 229–240.

Bower, G. H. (1972). A selective review of organizational factors in memory. In E. Tulving & W. Donaldson (Eds.), *Organization of memory*. New York: Academic.

Brener, R. (1940). An experimental investigation of memory span. *Journal of Experimental Psychology, 27*, 467–482.

Brown, E., & Deffenbacher, K. (1975). Forgotten mnemonists. *Journal of the History of the Behavioral Sciences, 11*, 342–349.

Brown, E., & Deffenbacher, K. (1988). Superior memory performance and mnemonic encoding. In L. K. Obler & D. Fein (Eds.), *The exceptional brain* (pp. 191–211). New York: Guilford.

Ceci, S. J., DeSimone, M., & Johnson, S. (1993). Memory in context: A case study of Bubbles P., a gifted but uneven memorizer. In D. J. Herrmann, H. Weingartner, A. Searleman, & C. McEvoy (Eds.), *Memory improvement: Implications for memory theory* (pp. 169–186). New York: Springer-Verlag.

Chase, W. G., & Ericsson, K. A. (1981). Skilled memory. In J. R. Anderson (Ed.), *Cognitive skills and their acquisition* (pp. 141–180). Hillsdale, NJ: Lawrence Erlbaum Associates.

Chase, W. G., & Ericsson, K. A. (1982). Skill and working memory. In G. H. Bower (Ed.), *The psychology of learning and motivation* (Vol. 16, pp. 1–58). New York: Academic.

Chase, W. G., & Simon, H. A. (1973). Perception in chess. *Cognitive Psychology, 4*, 55–81.

Corballis, M. C., Katz, J., & Schwartz, M. (1980). Retrieval from memory sets that exceed the memory span. *Canadian Journal of Psychology, 34*, 40–48.

Egan, D. E., & Schwartz, B. J. (1979). Chunking in recall of symbolic drawings. *Memory and Cognition, 7*, 149–158.

Ericsson, K. A. (1985). Memory skill. *Canadian Journal of Psychology, 39*, 188–231.

Ericsson, K. A. (1988). Analysis of memory performance in terms of memory skill. In R. J. Sternberg (Ed.), *Advances in the psychology of human intelligence* (Vol. 4, pp. 137–179). Hillsdale, NJ: Lawrence Erlbaum Associates.

Ericsson, K. A., & Chase, W. G. (1982). Exceptional memory. *American Scientist, 70*, 607–615.

Ericsson, K. A., Chase, W. G., & Faloon, S. (1980). Acquisition of a memory skill. *Science, 208*, 1181–1182.

Ericsson, K. A., & Faivre, I. A. (1988). What's exceptional about exceptional abilities? In L. K. Obler & D. Fein (Eds.), *The exceptional brain* (pp. 436–473). New York: Guilford.

Ericsson, K. A., Krampe, R. T., & Tesch-Romer, C. (1989, November). *Prudent practice makes perfect: An examination of elite violinists daily lives*. Paper presented at the meeting of the Psychonomic Society, Atlanta.

Ericsson, K. A., & Polson, P. G. (1988). A cognitive analysis of exceptional memory for restaurant orders. In M. Chi, R. Glaser, & M. Farr (Eds.), *The nature of expertise* (pp. 23–70). Hillsdale, NJ: Lawrence Erlbaum Associates.

Gates, A. I. (1916). The mnemonic span for visual and auditory digits. *Journal of Experimental Psychology, 1*, 393–403.

Gordon, P., Valentine, E., & Wilding, J. (1984). One man's memory: A study of a mnemonist. *British Journal of Psychology, 75*, 1–14.

Hanson, J. (1980, November). Numbers whiz tests limits of memory. *Report: A Publication for Faculty and Staff of the University of Minnesota*, pp. 6–7.

Hegge, T. (1918–1919). Beiträge zur analyse der Gedächtnistätigkeit, Über ungewöhnliche und illustrierende und lokalisierende Einprägung [Contribution to the analysis of the nature of memory for exceptional and illustrative and localized impressions]. *Zeitschrift für Psychologie, 84*, 349–352.

Holden, J. (1985). Ramanujan. *The names of the rapids.* Amherst: University of Massachusetts Press.

Horn, J. C. (1981, February). Memory II. *Psychology Today*, pp. 21, 80–81.

Hunt, E., & Love, T. (1972). How good can memory be? In A. W. Melton & E. Martin (Eds.), *Coding processes in human memory.* Washington, D.C.: Wiley.

Hunter, I. M. L. (1977). An exceptional memory. *British Journal of Psychology, 68*, 155–164.

Kintsch, W. (1974). *The representation of meaning in memory.* Hillsdale, NJ: Lawrence Erlbaum Associates.

Kucera, H., & Francis, W. N. (1967). *Computational analysis of present-day American English.* Providence, R.I.: Brown University Press.

Luria, A. R. (1968). *The mind of a mnemonist.* New York: Basic.

Meyer, D. E., & Schvaneveldt, R. W. (1971). Facilitation in recognizing pairs of words: Evidence of a dependence between retrieval operations. *Journal of Experimental Psychology, 90,* 227-234.

Morton, J. A. (1969). Interaction of information in word recognition. *Psychological Review, 76,* 165-178.

Morton, J. A. (1970). A functional model for memory. In D. A. Norman (Ed.), *Models of human memory,* New York: Academic.

Müller, G. (1911). Zur Analyse der Gedächtnistätigkeit und des Vorstellungsverlaufes, 1 [Toward the analysis of the nature of memory and its conceptualization, 1]. *Zeitschrift für Psychologie,* Erganzungsband 5, pp. 1-567.

Neely, J. H. (1976). Semantic priming and retrieval from lexical memory: Evidence for facilitatory and inhibitory processes. *Memory and Cognition, 4,* 648-654.

Neisser, U. (1964). *Cognitive psychology.* New York: Appleton-Century-Crofts.

Newman, J. R. (1956). Srinivasa Ramanujan. In J. R. Newman (Ed.), *The world of mathematics.* New York: Simon & Schuster.

Osterrieth, P. A. (1944). Le test du copie d'une figure complexe [A test for the reproduction of a complex figure]. *Archives of Psychology, 30,* 206-356.

Pelligrino, J. W. (1971). A general measure of organization in free recall for variable unit size and internal sequential consistency. *Behavioral Research Methods and Instrumentation, 3,* 241-246.

Rey, A. (1942). L'examen psychologique dans les cas d'encephalopathie traumatique [A psychological examination of a case of head injury]. *Archives of Psychology, 28,* 286-340.

Rice, G. E. (1980). On cultural schemata. *American Ethnologist, 7,* 152-171.

Roenker, D. L., Thompson, C. P., & Brown, S. C. (1971). Comparison of measures for the estimation of clustering in free recall. *Psychological Bulletin, 76,* 45-48.

Rubenstein, H., Garfield, L., & Millikan, J. A. (1970). Homographic entries in the internal lexicon. *Journal of Verbal Learning and Verbal Behavior, 9,* 487-494.

Rubenstein, H., Lewis, S. S., & Rubenstein, M. A. (1971). Homographic entries in the internal lexicon: Effects of systematicity and relative frequency of meanings. *Journal of Verbal Learning and Verbal Behavior, 10,* 57-62.

Sandor, B. (1932). Die Gedächtnistätigkeit und Arbeitsweise von Rechenkünstlern [The nature of memory and operating procedure of an arithmetic genius]. *Charakter, 1,* 47-50.

Shanks, D., & Wrench, J. W., Jr. (1962). Computation of pi to 100,000 decimals. *Mathematics of Computation, 16,* 76-99.

Sternberg, S. (1966). High-speed scanning in human memory. *Science, 153,* 652-654.

Susukita, T. (1933). Untersuchung eines ausserordentlichen Gedächtnisses in Japan, 1 [Investigation of an extraordinary memory in Japan, 1]. *Tohoku Psychologia Folia, 1,* 111-134.

Susukita, T. (1934). Untersuchung eines ausserordentlichen Gedächtnisses in Japan, 2 [Investigation of an extraordinary memory in Japan, 2]. *Tohoku Psychologia Folia, 2,* 15-42.

Taylor, E. M. (1959). *Psychological appraisal of children with cerebral defects.* Cambridge: Harvard University Press.

Thompson, C. P., Cowan, T. M., Frieman, J., Mahadevan, R. S., Vogl, R. J., & Frieman, J. (1991). Rajan: A study of a memorist. *Journal of Memory and Language, 30,* 702-724.

Thompson, C. P., & Roenker, D. L. (1971). Learning to cluster. *Journal of Experimental Psychology, 91,* 136-139.

Tulving, E. (1962). Subjective organization in the free recall of "unrelated" words. *Psychological Review, 69,* 344-354.

Vicente, K. J. (1988). Adapting the memory recall paradigm to evaluate interfaces. *Acta Psychologica, 69,* 249-278.

Weinland, J. (1948). The memory of Salo Finkelstein. *Journal of General Psychology, 39,* 243-257.

Wilcox, R. R. (1992). Why can methods for comparing means have relatively low power, and what can you do to correct the problem? *Current Directions in Psychological Science, 1,* 101-105.

Author Index

149

Subject Index